SERBIA: Faces & Places

Vladeta Rajić with Bill Dorich

Published in the United States by GM Books, Los Angeles, California.
Library of Congress Cataloging-in-Publication Data

Vladeta Val Rajić with Bill Dorich
SERBIA: FACES & PLACES

Distributed by:
GMBOOKS
P.O. Box 5310
Beverly Hills, CA 90209
(310) 475-2988 Fax (310) 475-2507

Website
www.SerbiaFacesAndPlaces.com

Internet Orders
www.gmbooks.com

ISBN #1882383-75-3
2 4 6 8 9 7 5 3 1

FIRST EDITION

Cover and Book Design: Bill Dorich and Mark Heliger
Editing: Cliff Carl and Anita Dorich
Book Production: Mark Heliger
Project Director: Anita Dorich
Photography:
Val Rajić and Bill Dorich,
Branislav Strugar
Katarina Stefanović
Russell Gordon

Printed in the USA
By Lithocraft Company, Anaheim, California

Foreword

SERBIA: Faces & Places is a book to make you feel good about being Serbian.

With dysfunctional geo-political policies imposed by outside powers in the Balkans and misrepresentation of Serbia in the Western media, it is rare today to find something to make American Serbians feel good about being Serbian or to understand the essence of being Serbians if you are a not one of them.

Vladeta (Val) Rajić, who emigrated from Serbia to America with his parents when he was eight years-old, has written and compiled a book of photographs with Bill Dorich, a first-generation American, that make you proud to be an American Serbian.

Mr. Rajić, in visiting the country of his birth, has spent countless hours and traveled thousands of miles to portray the ordinary hard-working people of Serbia. He depicts with love and passion the similarities between Serbians in the homeland and Serbians in America. It is a remarkable connection with our Serbian culture and heritage.

The authors explored nature's wonders, museums, historic places as well as important churches and monasteries. They not only recounted the discoveries of the spirit of the people of Serbia which inspired them to write this book, but they also produced an inspirational album of over 500 pictures and vignettes for all of us to enjoy. The pages exude the soul and heartbeat of Serbia.

Whether capturing the tempo of Belgrade, life on the farm, or reconnecting with his ancestry in Kragujevac and Bistrica, Mr. Rajić adeptly highlights the Serbian "Slava" and "family values which are the central element of our Serbian identity."

Val Rajić and Bill Dorich point out that Serbians revere their Eastern Orthodox Christian faith and they love to party at numerous festivals. They look to the future optimistically as Serbians display their entrepreneurship in small businesses, respect the importance of education and make us all proud because of their accomplishments and survivorship under adverse conditions.

Alex Machaskee
Retired President and Publisher
The Plain Dealer, Cleveland, Ohio
Ohio's Largest Newspaper

Table of Contents

Dedication

This book is dedicated to my parents. My father, Tihomir, has been very supportive of this project and even admits to having learned some things about Serbia as a result of this book. My mother, Zagorka, passed away a few years ago; however, I am sure she would have approved of my efforts in exposing Serbia and her people to a wide audience. It was because of my parents that I did not lose the connection with my heritage and culture and for that reason I also dedicate this book to the honest and hardworking people of Serbia. Their persevering spirit is inspirational. In the face of difficulties brought on by both friend and foe, the Serbian people never doubted that better days would be with them. In order to have some understanding of their true spirit of optimism, one only need remember that Belgrade's citizens, in the 20th century alone, endured *five* separate, lethal, organized and sustained aerial bombing attacks at the hands of foreign aggressors.

— *Vladeta Rajić*

As a journalist I have spent 20 years writing about and defending Serbia, including over 300 radio and television interviews and directly participating in various charities to aid hundreds of thousands of Serbian refugees forced to flee to Belgrade from Croatia, Bosnia and Kosovo. This book is dedicated to the Serbian people whose enduring tenacity made it possible for Serbs to survive centuries of foreign occupation and 5 wars in the 20th century—their will to survive; their enthusiasm for freedom; commitment to their faith; pride and work ethic, is the heart and soul of this book.

—*Bill Dorich*

Acknowledgments

After numerous trips to Serbia over the years and taking countless pictures, I would always remind myself that if I ever did a book about Serbia "that picture would have to be included." Having said that hundreds of times in hundreds of places throughout Serbia I met a fellow Serb with as much passion about Serbia as my own. To my great benefit Bill Dorich is a publisher in Los Angeles. Not being a professional photographer, I was a bit hesitant in sharing my pictures and my idea, but Bill quickly convinced me that I had the seeds of a wonderful book in which I could share my passion with a world-wide audience, including my friends and relatives in Serbia. Some of the images in this book were taken with my trusty Sony digital camera.

There are many wonderful images in this book which were contributed by Bill Dorich. His trip to Serbia with me in August, 2010 and the countless hours that he dedicated to designing the book are greatly appreciated and his contribution has turned my dream into a beautiful reality. Anita Dorich expertly directed the entire project and made a valuable contribution by ensuring the uninterrupted flow of the material for a successful outcome.

An additional element that made this book project possible was a total lack of understanding on my part of the required time commitment necessary to finish this work and how many behind-the-scenes helpers make a book possible. However, once started, I realized that the project had to be published as there is no other book in print that reveals the great visual pleasures that one will find in Serbia and how important it was to me to share my enthusiasm.

I also need to take the time and the space here to also pay tribute to the following people: Jasmina Savić and Marina Filipović, post-graduate students at the University of Illinois, for helping with writing, translation and research. In addition to directly assisting on this project, there are many others who have assisted by contributing ideas, suggestions, advice, encouragement, proofreading, or making introductions to special sources of help. Their contributions have been invaluable. Thank you Alex Machaskee, Dr. Srdja Trifković, Ken Pavichevich, Ben Hurwitz, Bob Pinzur, Carl Marcyan, Danny Smith, Djordje Mišković, Ivana Rajić, Vukman Krivokuća, Slavka Drašković, Deacon Aleksandar Sekulić, Eileen Mahoney Philbin, Maja Savić, Alex Dimitrijević, General Consul of Serbia Desko Nikitović and a special thank you for the hospitality of HRH Crown Prince Aleksandar and his office staff. Additionally a thank you to the Tourist Organizations of Niš, Subotica and Novi Sad. Last but equally important are all those who agreed to be my Faces for this project. If I have forgotten to include someone, and I probably have, my sincere apologies.

One individual requires a special word of gratitude and that is my daughter Margaret. Her patience with her father during one of our trips to Serbia in which she had to endure hot days of riding in the car, going from location to location, so that I could include some additional images or retake other pictures I was not pleased with. Though she never complained, I'm sure she would have rather been reclining in a hammock in the shade of the two giant cherry trees at her grandfather's mountain retreat in Bistrica.

Introduction

It was in the early 60s when my parents decided to emigrate from what was then known as Yugoslavia to the United States. They lived a middle-class lifestyle in the city of Kragujevac, Serbia which, after its destruction during World War II, was becoming economically revitalized and once again a vibrant industrial city. It was not economic hardship, a lack of freedom of expression, or Tito's Communist regime that motivated my family to move outside of the borders of their homeland. Their reason was different. Interestingly enough, it was the chronic and petty corruption in my father's place of employment which drove my family to seek a better future elsewhere.

I was 8 years old when our family started over in the United States. I grew up in a typical urban blue collar neighborhood on Chicago's northwest side, working part-time jobs after school and summers. I still maintain strong friendships from those early days when I did not have a good command of the English language.

Life became complete when I met my love in college, got married and we had our child. Years passed by quickly! I changed careers and employers several times and we saved for our child's education and our retirement.

There is one event, however, which has stayed with me and changed my life in many ways. It took place at a kids' birthday party in the late 90s. A gentleman in his sixties, an attorney with a successful law practice, approached me with a rather unusual question. He asked me, "Do you get together and celebrate birthdays like this back in Serbia?" I was so surprised by the question that the only thing I could answer was, "Yes ... we do." Although it was kind of him to be curious and to inquire about another culture, I realized at that moment that he had no notion of who I was or where I came from. His question stayed with me for a very long time and eventually motivated me to take a detailed look at the place where my family came from, its people, culture, history, conflicts, and how they are reflected in me. I am very grateful to the gentleman who asked me the birthday question because it helped me to rediscover the country of my birth. As I began making several trips to Serbia, I consciously made an effort to look beyond the surface of what I saw. My aim was to chronicle what I experienced at a more than typical tourist level. I realize that most people in the United States have very little knowledge about Serbia. My hope is that my observations provide a concise and representative picture of Serbia and its people to all those curious minds who want to learn a bit about this small country and its rich heritage and culture.

Serbs are genuine, hardworking, honest and generous people. Their values, dreams, and aspirations are familiar to all of us. They seek a better life and future for their children and grandchildren. But one should also appreciate that their frame of reference when approaching life is very different from that of most Americans or Western Europeans. It has to be; their history is responsible for this difference. Serbs were slaves, under Turkish occupation for 5 centuries, for whom education, literacy and music were virtually banned. History was passed on through poetry and storytelling. Many churches were turned into stables by Turkish invaders. Once the Ottoman rulers were defeated and expelled, new occupying powers arrived from the Austro-Hungarian Empire, Bulgaria and Germany. All of this left a profound impact on the Serbian people and their culture.

As I traveled through Serbia, I made an effort to take a closer look at the ordinary working people, their aspirations and dreams, their perspective of the past, the present and the future.

Quite a variety of individuals have had the opportunity to preview the manuscript of *SERBIA: Faces & Places*. It is interesting to me that the impression of all of those who have gone through the final drafts is fairly consistent; they all left with the feeling that they were much more similar to the Serbian people than they had realized.

May you enjoy my observations about my beloved Serbia.

Faces of Serbia

It's rather remarkable how little the average European or American knows about Serbia, its people or its rich culture and heritage. In the middle ages, before the onset of 5 centuries of Turkish occupation and enslavement, the Serbian Kingdom was one of the most powerful in Central Europe and the Balkans.

While the history of the most recent 5 centuries has not always been kind to the Serbian people, they have endured, survived, and even at times thrived under adverse circumstances. Many of them will tell you that it was their faith in God and Orthodox Christianity that helped them remain optimistic about a better tomorrow.

In meeting these people, it was interesting to notice that each had his or her own individual mission or dream, often guided and encouraged by family and friends. Although each of the people here is pursuing a different dream down a separate path, the same theme was heard loud and clear. Without exception, the goals and aspirations were to succeed personally so that their children and grandchildren could live a better life tomorrow. They are proud of their past, dating back to the middle ages, sad about the recent past because it is generally seen as an opportunity wasted, and hopeful about the future.

One of the real treats in visiting Serbia is the opportunity to get to know some of these people by simply striking up a conversation at a green market, city park, a café, or a bus stop, a museum or a monastery. Serbs are a social people. They are very well informed, very open and easy to engage in conversation, whether they are a taxi driver, teacher, police officer, farmer, government official, a student or shop owner. The following pages chronicle some of these interesting individuals. Sometimes conversation stumbles upon a topic, which, for an American or Western European, might be a bit uncomfortable. For instance, being asked about one's personal finances, which many consider private. However, the rural population is less inhibited in discussing those topics amongst themselves—and that is reflected in questions sometimes asked of strangers. It is all part of the experience of being in Serbia.

The general impression of Serbia's society is one of a shared value system with the rest of Europe and the United States; that is to say that the drive for success is primarily motivated by a desire for a better future for their children and grandchildren. However, it is also worth noting that Serbia is not a monolith and generalizations about the entire society do not apply. For example, the urban dweller in Serbia has more in common with their urban dwelling counterpart in Chicago or Munich than their own countrymen from the countryside. The same can be said of the non-urban population and their counterparts in the United States and Western Europe. In the end, it is truly remarkable how closely aligned are the dreams and aspirations of these people with those of their European and American brothers and sisters.

Serbia's Future

The young minds of Serbia's future leaders are being shaped in urban and rural schools. These are some of their creative works.

VIII
ИКОНОГРАФИЈА ·МОЗАИК·

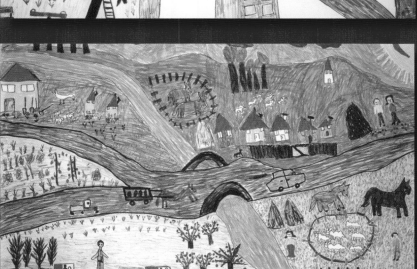

Families

Serbian people have always placed special importance on the family. Through the different historical circumstances and hardships (such as frequent wars and foreign domination) living in large family units consisting of several generations including in-laws, cousins and many children, helped Serbians survive and maintain their personal and national integrity. Over the course of time the family became a central element of the Serbian identity. The modern Serbian family, though quite a bit smaller, typically consisting of parents and one or two children, still maintains strong relationships and closeness among the family members. The family represents the foundation of society.

Families in Serbia tend not to be dispersed throughout the country, as in some parts of the world, which results in many families living in close proximity to other family members. All generations frequently remain in close contact and supportive relationships with one another. In fact, it is not unusual for four generations of cousins, uncles, aunts, and other family members to see each other every few days. They usually gather to have meals together and enjoy long conversations in a great family atmosphere. This characteristic pattern is perceived as an inherited family value that is most likely to be repeated by several generations. Helping to keep the family tradition alive, virtually every single household in Serbia celebrates its own family Patron Saint's Day, called Slava, which is passed on from generation to generation. The origins of Slava, or Krsna Slava, are said to date back to the time when Serbs accepted Christianity in the 8th or 9th century. At that time, entire villages would take part in mass baptisms which were performed on religious holidays. The holiday on which one's family accepted Christianity by taking part in one of these mass baptisms is the day the family would adopt as its Slava. Thus, for example, if someone celebrates Slava on St. Nicholas Day, it most likely means that their ancestors accepted Christianity by having taken part in a village-wide baptism on St. Nicholas Day well over a 1,000 years ago. Celebrating Slava with family members and friends symbolizes an everlasting image of Serbian family unity.

21

Family Farms

According to agricultural experts, about 90 percent of Serbia's arable land is owned by farmers running small family farms of 4 or 5 hectares. About 50 percent of Serbia's population lives in rural areas, many of whom make their living on small family farms. The other 50 percent have a close relative who lives on a farm.

These small family farms have been instrumental in helping the urban dwellers survive during difficult times by providing access to low cost produce, fruit and dairy products at urban farmers' markets, or, more directly for those with relatives still living on a farm. Sadly, many of these small farms are becoming extinct as the young people move to the urban centers and the elderly become too frail to work their own farms. It is not unusual for family members living in the cities to come back and help their relatives during certain periods when specific seasonal work needs to be done, such as during the grain harvest, fruit picking, or winter feed preparation for the cattle. As the elderly pass away, many rural homes and farmhouses are left vacant. As a result, many rural schools do not have enough students to remain open. The Serbian government has recently initiated a program of financial incentives to aid the revitalization of the small family farms, including the promotion of rural tourism. So far the results have been modest, but encouraging.

Desa

Baba Jela

Kosa

Desa runs the family farm by herself in Bistrica. Her husband passed away in the mid 1980s and her two children have moved to the city. She looks after two cows, a pig and about 20 chickens. With her vegetable garden and animals she is almost self-sufficient regarding food, only having to buy flour and sugar for baking needs.

Jela was a new bride in Bistrica when World War II broke out. She and her busband raised four children and have ten grandchildren and many great grandchildren. Her husband passed away a number of years ago and Baba Jela died in 2006.

Kosa has lived on a farm in Bistrica her entire life. She and her husband, who passed away in the early 1990s raised three children, two boys and a girl. Although retired, Kosa still works on her farm, especially during the summer months when there are many chores. She is helped by her sons, one of whom lives in Bistrica, and the other one in Nova Varoš, who comes to help his mom whenever he has time. Kosa's one big wish is that her grandchildren were able to visit her in Bistrica more often.

Rada

Brane

Rada and her husband have lived on a farm their entire life, raising a son and a daughter. It is not an exaggeration to say that her natural raspberry and wild strawberry juices, plus her buckwheat pie and buckwheat crepes would impress even Martha Stewart.

Brane worked on the family farm in Bistrica with his father, taking over the farm and the responsibility for taking care of his mother when his father passed away recently. A smart horse trader, both figuratively and literally, he and his wife raised a son and daughter and are proud grandparents to five grandchildren.

Velibor and Jovanka live on their small farm near Nova Varoš. They raised two daughters who are both married and have children of their own. They are warm genuine people who beam with pride when talking about their grandchildren.

Velibor and Jovanka

31

34

Serbia is blessed with the glorious gift of bountiful fruit. Fertile soil and excellent climate conditions are responsible for Serbia's rich colors, scents and tastes of its fruits and vegetables. Serbia is well known for growing many varieties of organic fruit, primarily on the small family farms. The results are quite spectacular.

Plums are among the most prevalent of the fruit grown in Serbia. Over the years plums became an unofficial symbol of Serbia and are often referred to as "Serbia's blue gold." They are sold fresh, pruned or processed. They are also used in producing Serbia's well known plum brandy, locally known as *šljivovica*. In addition to plums, Serbia produces very high quality blackberries, blueberries, sweet and sour cherries, grapes, apples, pears, apricots and peaches. Many varieties of jams and preserves are offered to foreign and domestic markets. Particularly popular are the fruit juices. When visiting Serbia, the excellent quality and variety of juices one encounters is always a pleasant surprise. Serbia is also well known as one of the leading producers and exporters of raspberries, most of which are grown on the small family farms.

This wealth of nature and human effort can also be found at open green markets throughout Serbia. No matter how good or bad the times are, these nature's wonders will always brighten one's day.

Beautiful Prairie Herb Grasses

When one sees the numerous meadows and pastures with their many varieties of flowers, grasses and herbs, it becomes easy to understand how this land can produce some of the healthiest and most flavorful organic foods. These beautiful fields with their herb grazing grasses produce the most flavorful cow's milk one can imagine. There is no more natural or healthy source of food for the cows, sheep and goats than these incredible grazing pastures. The milk here has a natural hint of sweetness which is very delicious and difficult to describe. That full flavor is carried over when cheeses and creams are produced from the milk.

In a conversation with a farmer in Western Serbia the discussion led to me asking him if tea was popular in Serbia. His response, which I think was half serious and half joking: "We don't drink teas, we just drink our milk instead!" A clever, yet disarming answer.

Bistrica is a village in Western Serbia, located halfway between Nova Varoš and Prijepolje, not far from Mileševa Monastery. Just as Vuk Karadzić expressed his love for his hometown of Tršić, I must say that, although not born in Bistrica, I think it is one of the most beautiful places on the face of the earth. It is a place where the special feelings for me extend beyond mere physical beauty, but also to the emotions I feel when I remember that my ancestors have been in this place for perhaps more than three, four or five hundred years.

As a youngster, I recall listening to stories of the struggles endured by my ancestors: The story of my grandfather who had to get permission from the occupying Turkish authorities so that he could keep several pigs; or the story of my great grandfather, Fr. Petar an Orthodox Priest in the mid 1800s under the Turkish occupation; or the story of the near execution of all the inhabitants of Bistrica by the Nazis during the German occupation. This event is particularly harrowing. It seems that a German motorcycle patrol was late in coming back to their local headquarters. The Nazi officers thought that the locals had ambushed and killed them, so they rounded up everyone in the village (except for two of my uncles and my father who was four years-old at the time and who hid in an attic of one of the buildings) and lined them up by the school building to execute them. Within minutes of that near tragic event, the two soldiers were found. They'd had an accident on the road and had been lying in a ditch with injuries. The German practice at that time was to execute 50 civilians for each German soldier who was wounded, and execute 100 civilians for each German soldier who was killed. It is an incredible feeling to think that everything I know about this place and all the people in it came within minutes of perishing.

Radojica

Radojica was born in Rutoši, near Priboj, where he lives today. Now retired, he spent more than six years of his working life on an excavation project for a tunnel which was constructed in connection with the local hydroelectric plant. His two sons, much to his delight, live nearby. One of the events Radojica never misses is the local country fair where he has an opportunity to see many of his old friends.

Stanimirka

Stanimirka is a remarkable lady. In spite of leading a difficult life she always has a warm smile on her face and a kind word for everyone. Her husband passed away in the late 1990s. A few years prior to that, Stanimirka's son was arrested and briefly jailed for taking part in a political opposition demonstration in the late 1980's. Retired now, she spends her leisure time traveling with tour groups as a tourist and looking after the family farm in Bistrica.

Nikola

Nikola, just like his boyhood idol, Nikola Tesla, works in the field of electricity. He is a technician at the hydroelectric dam near Priboj. In his spare time he helps his mother run the family farm. He has a particular talent for developing slight variations on locally grown fruit. Upon retirement he plans to devote more time to his passion for agriculture. He recently acquired several bee colonies and is also focusing on organic honey production for his own personal and family use.

Kristina

Jelena

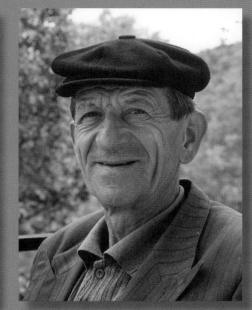

Nedeljko

Kristina was born in Nova Varoš but completed her higher education in Belgrade. Unlike many young people who go away to school in Belgrade, once Kristina finished her studies she decided to start her career in her home town. As a young banker, she devotes a lot of time to her work, while free time is spent mostly with her two sisters, or enjoying the unparalleled natural beauty of the Mt. Zlatar region.

Jelena was born in Bistrica near Nova Varoš and today lives in a beautiful area of Mt. Zlatar just above Nova Varoš near the ski slopes. Jelena is a full-time mom to her five children. Her husband does construction and maintenance work full-time. However, in the winter months he is a ski instructor at the nearby ski areas and also has a small ski rental business.

Nedeljko spent his entire career with a company in Nova Varoš which operates hotels and restaurants. He worked his way up from the bottom to a senior management role prior to his retirement. He now lives a completely different lifestyle. He and his wife stay busy playing with their grandchildren, growing raspberries and selling gourmet mushrooms. In his spare time, Nedeljko enjoys playing cards with his childhood friends.

Slavica

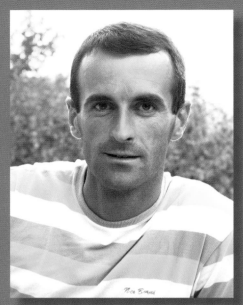

Vladimir

Ivan

Slavica typifies the resource-ful and self motivated people of Western Serbia. When the government owned company, for which she was an accountant, closed rather than wait around for a job to come along, she and her husband decided to sell their car and use the money to purchase equipment to open a coffee roasting, grinding and packaging business. At first things were difficult, but after a number of years the business has grown and is doing well. Slavica's brand of coffee, *Tajna*, can be found at virtually all the grocery stores, restaurants and cafés in the Nova Varoš area.

Vladimir grew up on his parents' farm in Bistrica near Nova Varoš. He works for a construction supply company in Nova Varoš. Recently married, he and his wife are planning to move to a house of their own and start a family soon. Even though, Vladimir has a full-time job, he still regularly helps his parents with their farm work in the summer months.

Ivan just received a text message and must meet his friends right away! He has finished school and is currently driving his own truck on international and domestic routes for a number of shipping customers. He lives with his parents in Nova Varoš, where he was born, while he saves up money for a place of his own. Being a fan of nice automobiles, one of his first purchases was a BMW which he enjoys driving.

Tihomir

Miroslav

Tihomir was born in Bistrica several years before the start of World War II. He still has vivid memories of how difficult life was during the war and the years which immediately followed. With the crops and livestock destroyed by retreating German troops, the years after the war were challenging in the most basic way; food was very scarce over the next few years. He finished trade school, became a tool and die maker and emigrated to the United States with his family in the 1960s. Upon retirement, Tihomir came back to his beloved Bistrica where he enjoys visiting with his relatives and pruning the trees in his fruit orchard. He has two sons, who with their families live in the United States. When he is bored, he jumps in his car and drives four hours in one direction to Belgrade in order to see his favorite soccer team play. He is happiest when his grandchildren from America come to visit him on the hill in Bistrica.

Miroslav was born in Bukovik in 1945 just as WWII was winding down. Upon earning a degree in economics in Belgrade, he spent his entire career in various senior finance roles at large firms. Miroslav's last job was that of president of the Nova Varoš branch of a large international bank. He and his wife, Mica, have two daughters. One followed her father's footsteps into banking and the other is a teacher. Now that he is retired, Miroslav is spending much more time with his four grandchildren, who make him very proud.

The Honey Festival in Nova Varoš

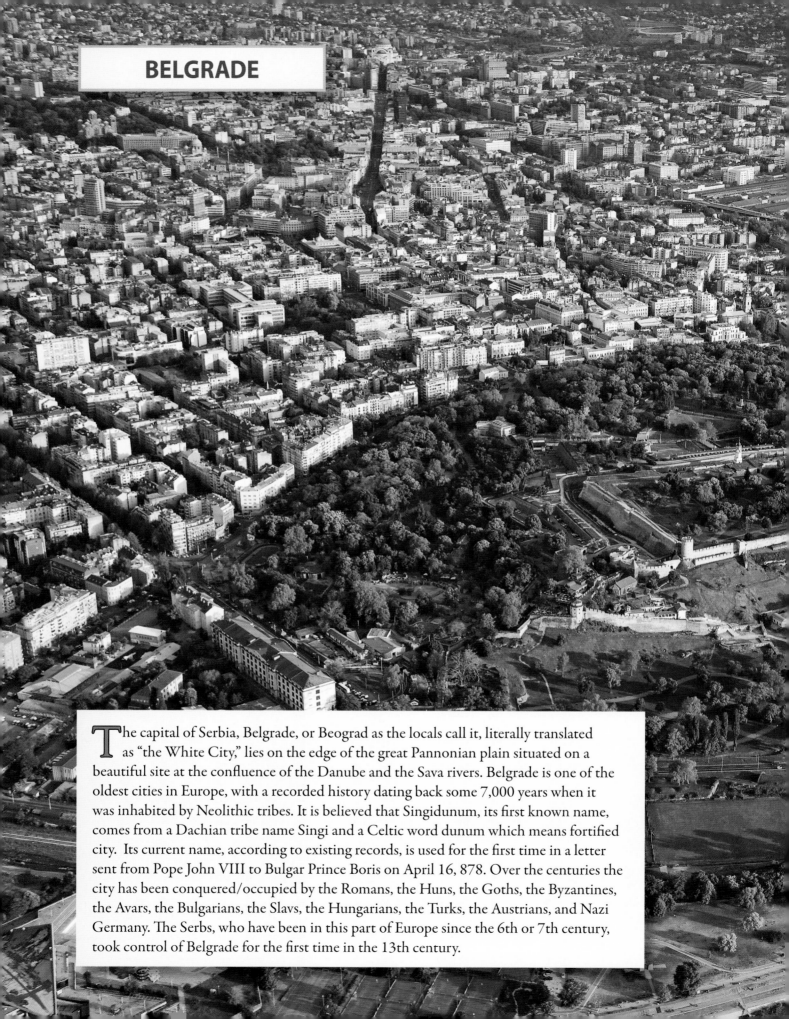

BELGRADE

The capital of Serbia, Belgrade, or Beograd as the locals call it, literally translated as "the White City," lies on the edge of the great Pannonian plain situated on a beautiful site at the confluence of the Danube and the Sava rivers. Belgrade is one of the oldest cities in Europe, with a recorded history dating back some 7,000 years when it was inhabited by Neolithic tribes. It is believed that Singidunum, its first known name, comes from a Dachian tribe name Singi and a Celtic word dunum which means fortified city. Its current name, according to existing records, is used for the first time in a letter sent from Pope John VIII to Bulgar Prince Boris on April 16, 878. Over the centuries the city has been conquered/occupied by the Romans, the Huns, the Goths, the Byzantines, the Avars, the Bulgarians, the Slavs, the Hungarians, the Turks, the Austrians, and Nazi Germany. The Serbs, who have been in this part of Europe since the 6th or 7th century, took control of Belgrade for the first time in the 13th century.

The statues in front of the Serbian Parliament are by sculptor Ivan Meštrović (1883-1962).

Belgrade Palaces, Old and New

There are two Palaces in Belgrade—the Old Palace (Stari dvor) and the New Palace (Novi dvor). Not to be confused with the Royal Palace and the White Palace.

If you are on a walking tour of the city center near Terzije Square you will see the Old Palace that houses the office of the Belgrade City Assembly. A park separates the the Palaces. The New Palace is the office of the President of the Republic of Serbia.

Belgrade's Botanical Gardens

Knez Mihailova Street

Belgrade Street Scene

Belgrade, like all European cities is a pedestrian's paradise. Belgrade is best explored on foot because virtually all areas can best be accessed this way.

❖ *Vlade Divac*

Vlade, born in Prijepolje and not far from the Mileševa Monastery, is an example of what is possible when someone makes it their mission to help those less fortunate than themselves.

Best known as a basketball superstar for his superlative playing in the NBA with several teams including the Los Angeles Lakers (for whom he was the first pick in the 1989 NBA draft) and Sacramento Kings, Vlade also competed in many international competitions where he represented Yugoslavia and Serbia with great personal pride. To list all of his professional accomplishments would require an entire page in this book.

Less well known, but in many ways much more important than his basketball successes, is his untiring devotion to helping the underprivileged. Together with his wife Ana, Vlade has been helping underprivileged children and catastrophe victims in the United States while he played in the NBA. More recently, upon retiring from basketball and moving back to Serbia, Vlade formed Humanitarian Organization Divac ("HOD") through which he and his wife have created a private program to help resettle the refugees and internally displaced persons in Serbia currently living in collective refugee centers. In 2010, HOD helped resettle 200 families (about 800 individuals in total) into their own apartments and houses by helping them buy and rehabilitate these properties. In some cases the aid has included helping these unfortunate people purchase tools and supplies in order to start small businesses or restart careers. HOD's goal for 2011 is to have the number of individuals resettled into their own homes exceed 4,000.

Vlade and Ana Divac will not consider their mission completed until all the refugee centers have been closed. These are truly special people who did not forget their heritage and continue to give back to their community.

Miloš was born and raised in Belgrade where he and his wife still live with their two daughters. Although he earned a degree in Economics at the university of Belgrade, his love of sports took his early career in a different direction when he became a sports columnist at a daily national newspaper. Subsequently, Miloš spent time in management with a major international hotel company. He currently heads the Belgrade office of an international executive recruiting and training firm as well as teaching university classes in hotel management. Both of his daughters play volleyball and like to spend their free time going to sporting events with their parents. The entire family enjoys traveling and regularly goes skiing.

Radmila was born in Užice. Upon graduating high school she continued her education at the university of Belgrade where she received her law degree. Radmila initially began building her career as an intern in the Circuit Court of Užice. Due to her dedication and hard work she soon became a Circuit Court judge. She was recently elected to the position of president of the High Court of Užice. Radmila was elected by a senior judicial council and she took her oath of office at the National Parliament. Although very happy with the contribution she is making to her profession, she has had a moment or two where down the road she can see herself as an Appellate Court judge in Belgrade. Radmila is a voracious reader and loves to travel.

Miloš

Radmila

Radovan

Milena

Upon completing his studies at the University of Belgrade, Radovan enrolled in the graduate business program at the University of Illinois in the United States, where he earned his MBA in finance. His early career was spent in banking with a major European bank. He was responsible for overseeing relationship management and business development in Central and Eastern Europe. In 2000 he left a senior banking position in order to answer the call of public service by joining the National Bank of Serbia. In 2004 he became the bank's Governor and served in that post until 2010. Governor Jelašić is fluent in four languages. He and his wife are the proud parents of three beautiful young children.

Milena is a native of Belgrade. She became a star of the Yugoslav Opera, making her operatic debut in 1989. She performed at the National Theatre in Belgrade for eight years in a wide range of roles. Milena then moved to Essen Opera in Germany where she earned the German Music Critic's Award as "Performer of the Season" for 1998. She has performed on some of the most prestigious stages in the world including: Germany, Austria, The Netherlands, Belgium, Czech Republic, Palm Beach, Washington, D.C., Los Angeles, The Metropolitan Opera and Carnegie Hall.

Skadarlija

No visit to Belgrade would be complete without a visit to Belgrade's well known and loved Skadarlija neighborhood. Only a few hundred meters from Belgrade's Republic Square, where the National Museum and the National Theatre are located, Skadarlija feels like a different world; a throwback to another time, when life was less hectic.

Skadarlija is named after Skadarska Street, a short, curving, pedestrian only cobblestone street which attracts large numbers of tourists. The main street is lined with many traditional Serbian restaurants (kafane), cafes, two hotels, art galleries, antique stores and souvenir shops. Many of these restaurants have open-air gardens and feature traditional live Serbian music. A short summer stroll through Skadarlija will have you experiencing a half dozen different local orchestras playing traditional Serbian songs at the various restaurants.

Skadarlija's traditions date back to the early years of the 1900s when the local establishments were well known for the prominent local and foreign writers, actors and poets who used to congregate there.

A few of these establishments such as Tri Šešira (Three Hats), Dva Jelena (Two Deer/Bucks), and Zlatni Bokal (The Golden Chalice) have survived and are still extremely popular with both locals and tourists. Many foreign dignitaries have visited these wonderful establishments when visiting Belgrade. Since 1993, the start of the summer season in Skadarlija has been marked with an official ceremony typically attended by celebrities, including popular singers and artists.

In 2008, plans were announced to reconstruct portions of Skadarlija in order to ensure that this urban oasis and its special atmosphere are not lost to uncontrolled development.

78

Jasmina

Marina

Vukman

Sometimes things are just meant to be. Marina and Jasmina accidently met in their first year of studies at Belgrade University. Each noticed that the other had a very unique but identical notebook. It was a notebook which had the logo of the Serbian post office on the cover and was available only to employees of the post office. It turned out that each of their fathers had given his daughter their work notebook to use in school. When they shared this news at home with their parents the pieces started to fall into place; their fathers, as it turned out, had known each other for many years. This event led to the two families becoming good friends and Marina and Jasmina becoming best friends. The authors of this book also are grateful for this pair who did the research for the religious and museum sections of this book.

Marina was born in Soko Banja, Jasmina in Belgrade. They both went to the same High School in Zemun and both majored in Serbian Language and Literature. Graduating from Belgrade University on the same day, each started working as Serbian Language teachers in Belgrade's public schools. After starting their teaching careers they each decided to pursue graduate degrees in Slavic Studies and both applied and were admitted to the Master's Degree program at the University of Illinois. In 2009, both received their graduate degrees in Slavic Studies. Marina and Jasmina have each decided to pursue a Ph.D. in Russian Language and Literature. In her spare time, Marina is an artist who enjoys painting, traveling and watching movies with friends. Jasmina's spare time is devoted to reading, researching Slavic folklore and writing. She is currently working on her first novel.

Vukman, born in Pirot, completed his education, including his university studies in economics, in Niš. Early in his career he led tour groups all over Europe for several travel companies. However, his deep love of art and culture started to be fulfilled when in 1991 he opened an art gallery in Niš. He operated the gallery until 2004 when he was named Assistant to the Minister responsible for economic cooperation with Serbia's Diaspora. More recently, in 2008 he became re-engaged in his love of culture when he was named Assistant to the Minister of the Diaspora responsible for issues dealing with culture, education, science and sports. Most recently, he was instrumental in the efforts to make available to Serbia's Diaspora the possibility to learning the Serbian language on the Web in an on-line environment. Vukman is fluent in several languages. He and his wife, a sociologist and librarian at the National Library in Niš, have two sons.

Milica

Aleksandra

Jelena

Milica was born in Užice. Following in her parents' footsteps, she graduated from Law School in Belgrade in 2008 and currently works as a staff attorney for the City of Belgrade. Having great communication skills and possessing strong leadership qualities, she is considering becoming either a criminal defense attorney or a prosecutor. Milica enjoys reading and traveling with her husband ... but only to sunny and warm locations.

After graduating from high school in Užice, Jelena did not follow in the footsteps of her parents, both of whom studied law, but rather enrolled in the economics program at the University of Belgrade. She completed her studies at the end of 2009 with special concentrations in the areas of banking and insurance. Jelena's hobbies are skiing, reading and traveling.

Aleksandra, born in Užice, wishes to continue the family tradition by attending Law School in Belgrade. Her mother is a Judge in Serbia's Judiciary and her father, who passed away a few years ago, also had a law degree. She is interested in economics and history as well as studying foreign languages (English and Spanish). In her spare time, Aleksandra enjoys skiing and traveling.

The Russian Tsar

The Russian Tsar, established in 1890, is a popular restaurant in Belgrade located centrally at Republic Square. Named after Russian Emperor Aleksandar II Romanov, the restaurant has over 20 portraits of the Emperor and is decorated in the Russian style depicting many events from Russian history. The Russian Tsar has always held an attraction for international visitors and especially for the locals to whom it serves as a symbol of Serbian-Russian friendship. Besides the excellent location, the Russian Tsar provides a pleasantly warm atmosphere in its romantic outdoor seating area and its very comfortable intimate indoor gallery. Although offering a fine selection of international and domestic cuisine and pastries, the real magic of this establishment remains the location and the atmosphere.

Street Performers

A River Town!

With two great rivers, one on either side of the city, Belgrade has always been considered a key transportation hub in Southeastern Europe. Restaurants and night clubs dot the Danube and Sava River banks. The restaurant seen in the middle of this image is shown in a larger view at the bottom of the page with its picturesque path leading from the mainland.

Jaša

Jaša and his wife emigrated to Western Europe to seek better economic opportunity when they were young. However, the tug of the place where they were born was very strong. They returned to Mladenovac where Jaša looks after his fruit trees and enjoys being near friends and family.

Bane

Bane grew up on a farm. In the 70s he was a member of the first graduating class of the then newly formed Police Academy. He has previously owned and operated a coffee roasting business, but now Bane is excited about the car wash business he recently opened in Belgrade.

Branko

Branko is a teacher in Belgrade. His wife is a counselor with the Serbian Chamber of Commerce. They have two teenage children. Their daughter would like to be a musician and their son plans to study drama. Branko and his wife recently built a new house in Belgrade which has three apartments. When the children grow up and have families of their own, they will not have to face the challenge and expense of finding housing in Belgrade's expensive real estate market. In his spare time Branko is an avid hunter.

Jugana and Milica

Marijana and Ivana

Jugana and Milica are from Mladenovac and have a typical good mother-daughter relationship. Jugana and her husband are blessed with two beautiful children and her mom Milica could not be a happier grandmother.

Marijana and Ivana are cousins. Both are from Nova Varoš and together they ended up in Belgrade in pursuit of a higher education and a career. Marijana, recently married and a new mother, is an accounting manager for an international firm in New Belgrade and Ivana recently received her M.S. degree in engineering. She now works in the telecommunication department of a major corporation in Obrenovac, near Belgrade, where she is a rising young star.

Kalemegdan at Night

As impressive as Kalemegdan Fortress is in the daytime, it is very special and very serene at night. After an evening stroll through Kalemegdan Park, crossing Francuska Street will reveal the popular pedestrian street Knez Mihailova. A short walk from there is the *"?" Restaurant*, the oldest continually operating restaurant in Belgrade. It dates back to the early 1800s. The story of how it acquired its name is a fun research project for anyone visiting Belgrade.

An Island Oasis in a Bustling City
ADA CIGANLIJA

An oasis in the center of Belgrade on the Sava River near where it flows into the Danube is the island of Ada Ciganlija, nicknamed "Belgrade Sea." It is covered in thick deciduous trees with ample open spaces for golf, family gatherings and in the summer, bicycling, along with first-rate sun bathing beaches. The area also offers various activities including water polo, rowing, kayaking, wind surfing, in addition to swimming. The more rigorous sports to enjoy are those such as wall-climbing and bungee-jumping. For those who like to fish the lake is well stocked with prize and rare fish of strictly controlled quality. Traditional restaurants abound by the water's edge, including numerous clubs and cafes popular with the younger generation especially during the summer months. In addition to the causeway from the city to Ada Ciganlija, a temporary pontoon bridge is provided from the mainland to The Great War Island seen below.

The Belgrade Zoo

Called Belgrade Good Hope Garden, the Belgrade Zoo was founded in 1936 and is one of the oldest zoological gardens in Europe. It is located in the heart of the city next to Kalemegdan Park. Interestingly enough, one side of the zoo is actually situated in the ramparts of the old Kalemegdan fortress. Currently, in the midst of a multi-year renovation, the zoo has an impressive collection of wild and domestic animals (over 2,000 animals representing about 200 different species). Of particular significance are the birds.

City of Statues

Belgrade is a city of statues. From the medieval period, the Karadjordje and Obrenović reigns, the Tito era and representations of Serbia's writers and poets, the statues are everywhere!

Vuk Karadzić

Vuk, often referred to as the father of the modern Serbian language, was born into a peasant family. He was taught to read and write by his cousin who was the only literate person in the region.

Vuk went on to reform the Serbian language by standardizing the form spoken by ordinary common people rather than using some of the other versions which had Russian and Church Slavonic influences. The quote most often attributed to him, but which actually was not his, is that one should "write as you speak and read as it is written." This is the essence of his philosophy and forms the basis of today's mostly phonetic Serbian language.

Vuk also greatly contributed to Serbian folk literature by compiling oral tales, poems, songs, proverbs and stories told by peasants. These then formed the foundation of his works. His works were highly regarded in Russia and Austria and so inspired Goethe that he was motivated to learn to speak Serbian. He encouraged Johannes Brahms to compose his famous lullaby based on a Serbian folk poem.

Vuk's legacy endures today. Although he died in Vienna, his remains were laid to rest at Belgrade's Cathedral Church next to his respected mentor Dositej Obradović.

Dositej Obradović

When Dositej boarded a boat for
Zemun on an August morning in
1807—his thoughts were consumed
with finally returning to Belgrade, never
realizing that this was going to be his last
trip in a life of uninterrupted short and
long journeys.

In the impatience of his youth he was
inspired to leave his birthplace in Banat
to take refuge in the Hopovo Monastery
on Mount Fruška Gora, arriving as a
young man named Dimitrije and leaving
as a monk named Dositej.

One of Serbia's most educated men
of the period, he returned to Belgrade
at the age of 70. Obradović came to
Serbia at the request of Karadjordje who
was about 10 years younger and called
him Uncle Dositej, most likely out of
respect for his wisdom and knowledge.
He spent his last few years in Belgrade
after the First Serbian Uprising that
liberated the Serbs from centuries of
Turkish rule. His famous remark was
"I grow old, learning." That love of
intellectual enlightenment has made
Dositej Obradović one of the foremost
reformers of modern Serbia.

He spoke eleven languages and
translated many European classics into
Serbian.

НА ОВОМ МЕСТУ ЈЕ 6/19 АПРИЛА
1867. г. ПРОЧИТАН ФЕРМАН
СУЛТАНА АБДУЛ АЗИСА КОЈИМ СУ
БЕОГРАДСКА, КЛАДОВСКА, СМЕДЕ-
РЕВСКА И ШАБАЧКА ТВРЂАВА
ПРЕДАТЕ НА УПРАВУ И ЧУВАЊЕ
КНЕЗУ МИХАИЛУ ОБРЕНОВИЋУ III
И СРПСКОЈ ВОЈСЦИ.

ПОВОДОМ СТОГОДИШЊИЦЕ.
У БЕОГРАДУ 1967. ГОДИНЕ.

Kalemegdan Park, the place where the Keys to Serbian towns were symbolically returned to Serbia.

At this location in April, 1867, the decree of Sultan Abdul Azis was read by which responsibility for the administration of and security for Belgrade, Kladovo, Smederevo and the Šabac Fortresses were transferred to Knez Mihailo Obrenović III and the Serbian Military.

The memorial was in commemoration of its centennial, Belgrade in 1967.

King Aleksandar I

Vojvoda Putnik

Vojvoda Mišić

Gen. Djurišić

Although most Serbians eagerly anticipate better times and a brighter future, a tour of Belgrade and much of Serbia reveals that Serbs have not forgotten—and in fact in some cases, revere their heroes from the past—most notably King Petar I, King Aleksandar I, Vojvoda Putnik, General Mišić, General Djurišić and others, as portrayed in these discretely placed plaques in one of Belgrade's city parks.

ВОЛИМО ФРАНЦУСКУ
КАО ШТО ЈЕ ОНА
НАС ВОЛЕЛА
1914-1918

Monument in Kalemegdan Park dedicated to France for
coming to the aid of Serbia in WWI.
Inscription reads: *We Love France Just as She Loved Us, 1914-1918*

Radoje Domanović

Djura Jakšić

Knez Miloš

109

Contrast: New Belgrade and the Old City Center

New Belgrade is located west and across the Sava River from the Old City Center of Belgrade. New Belgrade was built by clearing and filling a swampy plain in the years after WWII. The main characteristics of New Belgrade are highly contrasted to those across the river. The first visible differences include the flatness of New Belgrade that opposes a hilly terrain across the river; the street grid system compared to the more ad hoc city design so common to older urban areas; and a modernistic architectural style compared to the more classic ornamental approach of years gone by.

New Belgrade's contemporary architecture reflects 2 distinct periods in its development. The first is represented by the typical drab concrete apartment blocks from the period of the Communist era construction boom in the 1950s, '60s and '70s. The mandate at the time was to build as many housing units as quickly and as economically as possible. The goal was to settle as many people as was reasonable in very densely constructed neighborhoods. Because of this, the residential areas of New Belgrade in the 1980s were jokingly referred to as "dormitories." The second period, reflecting construction projects from the late 1980s onward, is typified by the glass and steel, modern and comfortable, but austere, structures such as apartment buildings, shopping areas, office towers and hotels which one normally can see in modern cities worldwide. Due to its wide open areas, New Belgrade is where much of the real estate development has taken place since the year 2000. New Belgrade is modern, clean, functional and efficient, but it lacks the grace and charm of the old city.

In contrast, across the Sava River and opposite New Belgrade is the Old City with its long, rich, and often destroyed architectural history. Belgrade has amazing architectural structures just like those in Budapest, Prague, or Vienna, though much fewer in number, as many buildings were destroyed during both World Wars. Because of this, besides Kalemegdan Fortress, which dates back to ancient times, the majority of Belgrade's buildings are from the 19th century. Still, diverse and rich, Belgrade's architecture has preserved many distinctive features from all periods of its evolution. Judging by the decorative elements—materials, shapes of windows and tops of buildings—one can keep track of all the major stages of expansion: Turkish (Vuk and Dositej Museum), Western influence (Captain Miša's Building), development of national architecture, adoption of foreign influences (National Theatre) and acceptance of different artistic movements.

Some of those represented are neo-Renaissance (National Bank of Serbia Building), academism influenced primarily by the Russian school of architecture (the buildings of the Main Post office and Patriarchy), neo-Byzantine style (the building of Ministry of Education). The diversity of architectural styles give a special charm and soul to the city in which the old merges with the new. Although it is difficult for the older buildings to compete with the new sterile structures in terms of efficiency and practicality, the Old City has a warmth and charm which never goes out of style.

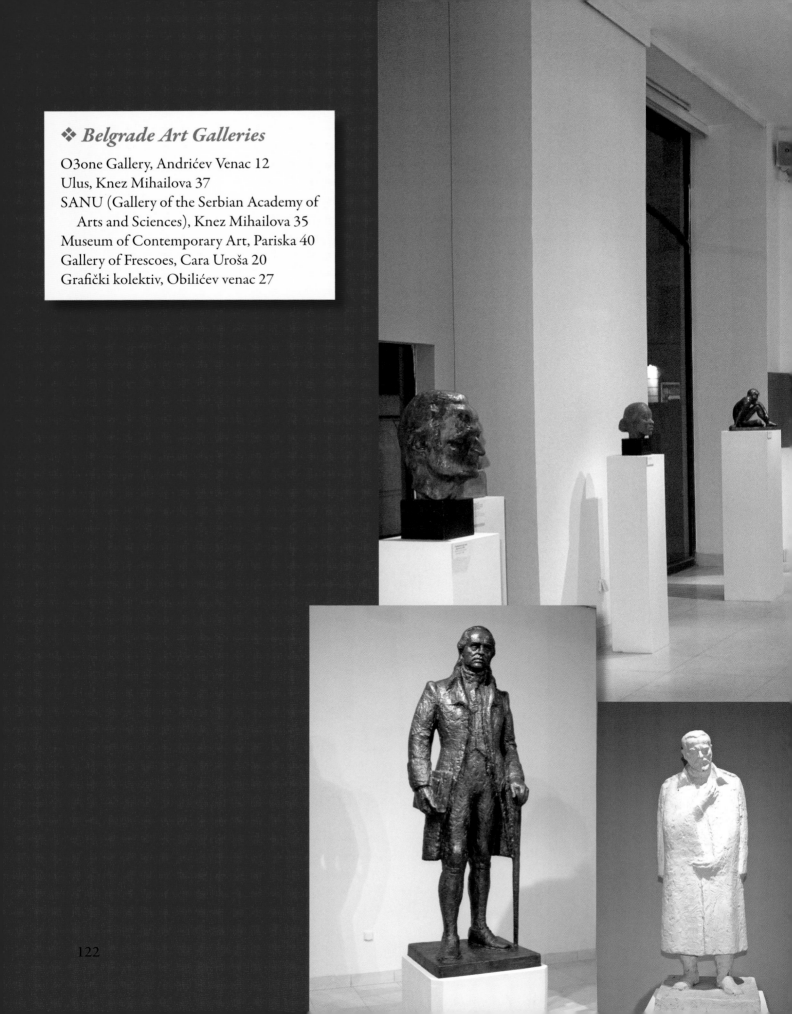

❖ *Belgrade Art Galleries*

O3one Gallery, Andrićev Venac 12
Ulus, Knez Mihailova 37
SANU (Gallery of the Serbian Academy of
 Arts and Sciences), Knez Mihailova 35
Museum of Contemporary Art, Pariska 40
Gallery of Frescoes, Cara Uroša 20
Grafički kolektiv, Obilićev venac 27

Fine Art

One of Serbia's most important artists is Paja Jovanović (1859-1957). Right: *The Cock Fight* and a nude of his wife. Below: *The Wedding of Tsar Dušan*, and his most famous painting: *The Great Migration*, depicting the 30,000 Serbian families who fled from Kosovo in 1690 and led by Patriarch Arsenije to escape Turkish reprisals. Painted by Jovanović in 1895, the original hangs in a prominent place at the Serbian Patriarchate in Belgrade.

Interior: Paja Jovanović Museum

Folk Art

The uniqueness of Serbian folk art is exemplified by the work of several local artists:

Miroslav Srećković

Dragica Galjić

Dušanka Petrović

Dejan Živanović

Milovan Lazarević

Regional art by Plavšić

Icon and Fresco Painting
—A tradition of devotion.

Priests and monks in monasteries throughout Serbia practice this ancient art form utilized by 280 million Orthodox Christians worldwide.

The Frescoes painted on the center dome of the small chapel on Vračar iconographically records the burning of the relics of St. Sava by the Ottoman Turks on this site in 1594, some 360 years after St. Sava's death. Intended to demean the Serbs and their continued worship of Sava, the burning of his relics intensified his place in Serbian history and Christian Orthodoxy. Below is a modern icon of St. Sava.

While the Belgrade Philharmonic Orchestra was founded rather recently—shortly after WWI, it quickly gained an excellent reputation and during the 1960s and 1970s was ranked by international experts as the 5th best in Europe. The Orchestra was practically dormant in the 1990s due to the severe economic situation brought on by the Balkan conflicts.

Beginning in 2000, the Belgrade Philharmonic Orchestra was fully operational, including hosting a full-season schedule and making numerous international appearances. Many young performers have joined, giving the Belgrade Philharmonic Orchestra a new and energized spirit and excitement.

Seen below is Gautier Capuçon performing in Belgrade with the Prague Symphony Orchestra in 2009.

Belgrade Philharmonic Orchestra   133

Robert Plant

Joe Cocker

John McLaughlin

134

Carlos Santana

Kenny Garrett Quartet

Serbian National Theatre

José Carreras singing with the Belgrade Symphony.

Serbian performance of Les Miserables

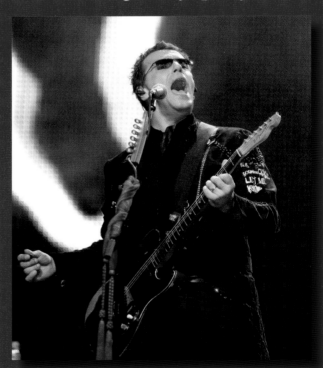

Serbian Rocker, Van Gogh

136

Serbian National Ballet, Swan Lake

Boban and Marko Marković

The Boban and Marko Marković Orchestra has been called the quintessential Balkan brass band. This 13 piece band draws its musical inspiration from many Balkan cultures but does not stray far from its Romani traditions. Boban and his orchestra have won many accolades including: "Leading Band in Serbia"; "Trumpet Maestro"; "Golden Trumpet"; "The Best Orchestra." They have toured throughout Europe and North America and have released more than a dozen albums. The orchestra's music has also been featured in Emir Kusturica's well known films "Underground" and "Arizona Dream."

Since 2006 Boban's son, Marko, has co-led the band with his father. Boban and Marko come from a family of musicians. Boban's father, Dragutin, as well as both of his grandfathers, were musicians. Growing up, Boban dreamed of becoming a professional soccer player. However, at age 10, his father sat him down and told him that his destiny was to be a trumpet player. He began playing professionally at age 16 and formed his own orchestra by the time he was 20 years old.

In 1984 Boban won the honor of "First Trumpet" at the prestigious Guča Trumpet Festival and since then has won that same honor 5 more times. The orchestra has a world-wide following. Boban is very pleased that Marko has joined and co-leads the orchestra because the Marković trumpet legacy will endure. Apparently, Boban's father, Dragutin, was right; his destiny was, indeed, to be a trumpet player.

The musical group **Legende** (Legends) formed by its guitarists, Zoran Dašić and Lazar Marin, has continued to be one of the most popular musical acts in Serbia. To date, they have performed in about 1,500 concerts and have produced a number of CDs. Their popularity extends far beyond the borders of Serbia, as they have performed internationally many times in Europe and North America. Their music is a beautiful mix of traditional love ballads, immersed in smooth yet complex and pleasing regional melodies, all of which is accomplished with a combination of traditional and non-traditional Serbian musical instruments. According to the band members, their intent is to have the traditional characteristics of Serbian music be maintained as we enter the 21st century. Although the music is entirely different in origin and character, the execution is reminiscent of the early work of the Beatles.

The group's 6 members had all achieved an impressive level of professional success prior to becoming members of Legende. One of the members was with the Belgrade Opera for 9 years, 2 were members of a professional choir, 2 were in the Belgrade Philharmonic, one is a member of a theatre company, one has written film scores, one is a professor of music, one was a member of the national orchestra for TV Belgrade, one was a music producer for Radio/TV Serbia, and one authored 2 books. These truly are very talented and impressive artists, whose music as part of Legende, is simply magical.

Lazar Ristovski was born in Ravno Selo in Vojvodina, Serbia and currently resides in Belgrade. He completed his University studies in Belgrade with degrees in education and dramatic arts with a concentration in acting. Early in his career he devoted his professional efforts to the theatre where he mastered a classical repertoire (Shakespeare, Moliere). His interpretations of Hamlet, Don Juan and Amadeus are well known. Additionally, he has performed roles from works of Serbian writers, the best known of which is Dušan Kovačević. His credits include more than 4,000 performances in all parts of former Yugoslavia.

He has played characters in more than 50 films, TV series and TV dramas primarily as the lead. He has worked with major directors such as Kusturica, Paskaljević and Marković. Lazar has played unforgettable roles—Crni (Blackie) in "Underground" and Raja in "Tito and Me." His self authored film project "White Suit" (Belo Odelo) had its premiere at the Cannes Film Festival in 1999.

Lazar Ristovski is one of the leading and most influential Serbian actors who has been recognized with numerous foreign and domestic awards. He owns and operates the Zillion Film production company.

The Royal Palace and the White Palace were built between 1924 and 1929 as the private residences of King Aleksandar I and King Petar II. Today the Royal Palace is the home of Crown Prince Aleksandar Karadjordjević and his wife HRH Princess Katarina. It is located in Dedinje, the most exclusive area of Belgrade. The new U. S. Embassy is being built on an adjoining parcel of land.

The main entrance hall is often used as a reception area for visiting international world leaders. The main floor consists of the Royal Dining Room, the Blue Salon and Library, authentically furnished. The Royal Palace houses an art collection that reaches the status of a national treasure. The lower level offers another reception room, a billiards room as well as a motion picture theatre. Tours are only available on Saturdays and Sundays and require a reservation.

The Palace exterior is representative of the Serbian-Byzantine architectural style while the interior combines several distinctive styles from different epochs. The Formal Entrance Hall is designed in medieval style decorated with reproductions of frescoes from the Serbian monasteries Dečani and Sopoćani. The Blue Drawing Room is decorated in the Baroque style while several other rooms, such as the Golden Drawing Room, the Library, the King's Cabinet and the Royal Dining Room, are decorated in the Renaissance style. The walls of the Royal Recreation Floor on the lower level are painted in a rather traditional manner with images from Russian fairy tales, the Persian tale of Scheherazade and illustrations from Serbian epic poems.

The Royal Palace compound is surrounded with a beautiful swimming pool, park terraces, pavilions and a concert platform and covers over 100 hectares. In addition, there are two more buildings which are also part of the Royal compound. One is the Royal Chapel dedicated to St. Apostle Andrew the First–the Patron Saint of the Royal Family. It is attached to the Royal Palace itself. The other structure is the White Palace, built as the residence of King Aleksandar I's three sons—Petar, Tomislav and Andrej. Within the compound and the two palaces is housed a priceless collection of paintings and sculptures by world-renowned artists. The incredible beauty of this property makes it a favorite destination of tourists visiting Belgrade.

HRH Crown Prince Aleksandar II
HRH Crown Princess Katarina

142

The Liberator

King Perar I was a remarkable man. Well educated, he committed himself to making Serbia a modern parliamentary democracy. King Petar I is known to have translated into the Serbian language Stuart Mill's "On Liberty." He reigned from 1903 to 1921. The king was immediately confronted with numerous political and international problems which the Austrian Empire exploited and which ultimately resulted in the outbreak of WWI. In 1914, during WWI, he transferred administrative powers to his son and heir apparent, Crown Prince Aleksandar, due to his failing health. In spite of his deteriorating health, King Petar I marched on foot with his troops during a retreat in the middle of winter across the Albanian mountains. This retreat set the stage for a subsequent counter-attack which liberated Serbia from the Austro-Hungarian and German occupiers. Belgrade was the first city lost in WWI and the first city recaptured by Serbian troops. Serbia paid a very high price in human casualties but the people of Serbia came to love and respect King Petar I as he had stayed with his people during this most difficult set of circumstances. Thus, this humble monarch had come to be known to his people as *The Liberator*.

King Petar I passed away in 1921 at the age of 77 at which time his son Crown Prince Aleksandar ascended to the throne as King Aleksandar I.

Paintings in the main dining room at the Palace include a portrait of King Petar I and his son King Aleksandar I, who suceeded him to the throne, and a painting of King Peter II that went missing for decades until a family friend discovered it in an antique shop in Venice and brought it back to Serbia.

Seen here on horseback is King Aleksandar I who was tragically assassinated, along with Louis Barthou the French foreign minister, on a state visit to France in 1934. Yugoslavia was temporarily ruled by the king's brother as his son, Crown Prince Petar, the heir to the throne, was not yet of age. Crown Prince Petar did ultimately accede to the throne as King Petar II, but was prevented from returning to his homeland after WWII by the communists. The Royal Family was stripped of their citizenship and their property was confiscated. King Petar II died in exile in the United States and remains the only Monarch to be buried on U.S. soil. His son, Crown Prince Aleksandar is the rightful heir to the throne.

The Monarchy was abolished by the communists in 1947 without a public referendum. Currently, the Crown Prince and his wife HRH Crown Princess Katarina live in Belgrade at the Royal compound and are engaged full time in charity work in Serbia. Crown Prince Aleksandar would like to see Serbia returned to its former status as a constitutional parliamentary monarchy.

The bottom image is that of the office of Prince Aleksandar.

*The room in which the late
Richard Holbrooke, U.S.
Assistant Secretary of State
and the late President
Slobodan Milošević discussed
military threats against Serbia.*

*The settee seen here is where
the threats to bomb Serbia
were delivered.*

The White Palace

Rembrandt and rare books are part of the extensive collection at the Palaces.

159

St. George Church at Oplenac

Built in the early 20th century by the Karadjordjević ruling dynasty, Oplenac is more than a resting place for the members of the Royal Family. It is one of Serbia's national treasures. The compound consists of St. George Church, the Karadjordje Museums and Karadjordje Park. The church was built on a spot chosen by King Petar I in 1903. As one enters the church, on the right side is a mosaic portrait of King Petar I holding the model of St. George Church in his hands. Next to this portrait there is an entire gallery of portraits of Serbian medieval rulers and the churches they built. Some of the most famous are Stefan Nemanja holding a model of Studenica Monastery, King Stefan Prvovenčani with his model of Žiča, Prince Lazar holding the model of Ravanica Monastery and King Milutin holding the model of Gračanica Monastery, all exquisitely presented in mosaic tile so skillfully crafted that they appear as paintings. This church also gives a post-mortal shelter to two historically significant tombs; one belongs to King Petar I and the other to Karadjordje, the leader of the First Serbian Uprising of 1804. This church is also the final resting place for 20 other members of the Karadjordjević family. Six generations of the Karadjordjević dynasty are buried here.

163

167

169

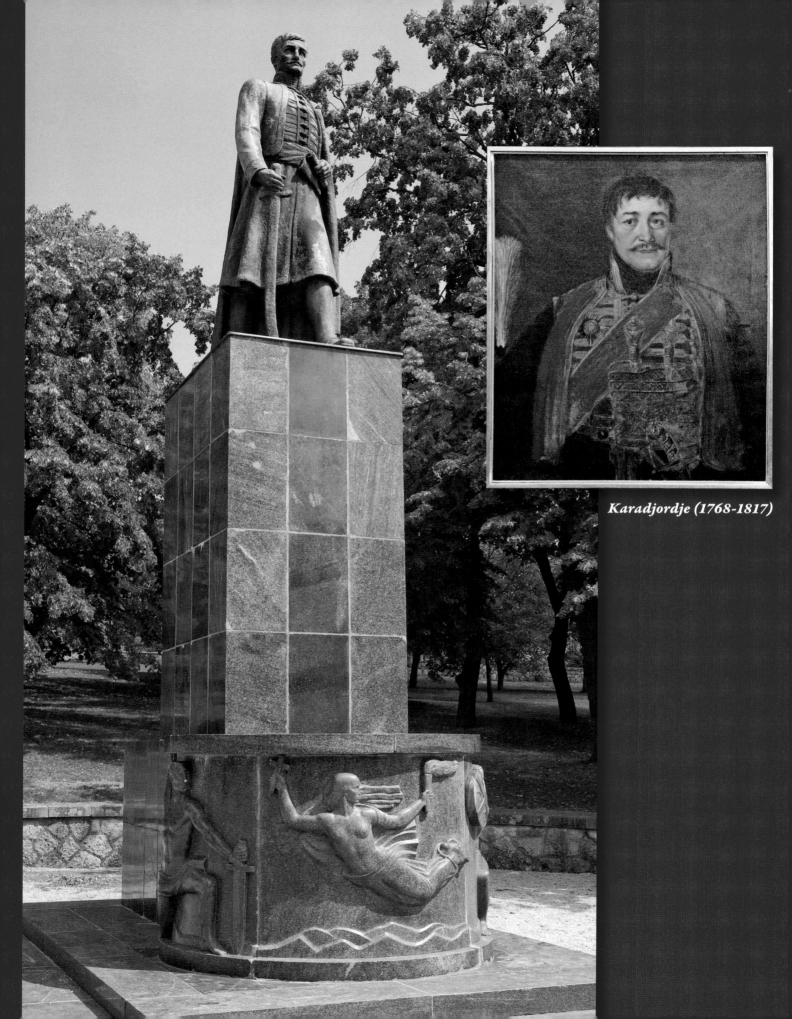

Karadjordje (1768-1817)

At the exit of the Oplenac complex there is a rather unassuming building which most visitors to Oplenac fail to visit. It is the former residence of the Royal Family's viticulturist. The building is now a museum housing an antique clock collection and a permanent exhibit of the works of the well known Serbian impressionist Nikola Graovac. Oplenac is a must-see for any visitor to Serbia.

Avala Tower

Mt. Avala is located about 30 minutes south of Belgrade and has an elevation of 1,677 feet above sea level. The locals refer to it simply as Avala. Being so close to Belgrade, Avala is one of the most popular summertime picnic destinations among the citizens of the capital. Its elevation provides a magnificent view of Belgrade. Special attractions of Avala are: the Monument to the Unknown Hero which is built in the form of a mausoleum to honor the unknown Serbian soldiers from WWI; Memorial Park dedicated to the victims of WWII; and the Avala TV tower which is noticed when first approaching the city from the west, south or east. The entire Avala area is a lush green national park with many recreational activities available to visitors.

The tower, measuring over 200 meters in height was originally completed in 1965 and had become an unofficial symbol of Belgrade. The tower housed TV transmission equipment and had an observation deck at the 135 meter level. It was the only tower in the world to have an equilateral triangle as its cross-section and one of very few to be standing on its tripod legs rather than being anchored into the ground.

In April, 1999, the Avala Tower was one of the last things destroyed by NATO before the bombing ceased. The tower's destruction was, according to NATO, meant to take the TV transmissions off the air. However, within minutes the broadcasting continued via a network of local transmission stations. Avala Tower is the third tallest structure in the world destroyed after the World Trade Center's twin towers in New York.

Avala Tower was rebuilt in 2009, to almost identical specifications as the original tower. Fund-raising efforts for rebuilding the tower commenced a few years after its destruction with early funding support provided by Serbia's tennis stars Novak Djoković and Ana Ivanović, seen on the following pages. The tennis stars memorialized these fund-raising events by placing their hand and foot prints at the site.

Today, Belgrade is proud to have its tower back.

Avala Monument

Monument to the Unknown Hero built in the form of a mausoleum to honor the unknown Serbian soldiers from WWI; Memorial Park is dedicated to the victims of WWII.

Novak Djoković

174

Ana Ivanović

MUSEUMS

The idea of establishing an institution which would protect and promote national cultural heritage was initiated in Serbia in the first half of the 19th century. This occurred as Serbia was fighting for, and successfully gaining, increased freedoms and autonomy from the occupying Turkish Empire. Thus, the first such institution, a predecessor to all Serbian museums, the National Museum, was founded in 1844. The very first collections of the museum focused primarily on the development and changes of societies on the territory of today's Serbia from the prehistoric to the medieval period. Over time, the museum's collections grew with the works of significant artistic styles and trends in national and world art. With the resulting lack of adequate space, at the end of the 19th and the beginning of the 20th century there was a great need for specialized museums. At that time Serbia undertook a program of establishing many of those museums across the country.

Today Belgrade, as a major European capital, boasts 35 museums. Unfortunately, the main building of the National Museum was closed for renovation at the time of the publishing of this book and except for several file images, could not be included in this section. Belgrade has many other museums worth seeing, some of which are highlighted in the pages to follow. In addition, there are many other valuable museums worth visiting including: the Railroad Museum, the Museum of Jewish Culture, the Museum of African Art, the Museum of Contemporary Art.

With more than 35 museums in Belgrade alone, one could easily spend weeks in Serbia touring just those.

The Gallery of Frescoes

As part of The National Museum, the Gallery of Frescoes was established in 1973. The Gallery is an art school dedicated to the mission of preserving the skill of the art of fresco. It is also a gallery, open to the public, featuring the work of the school's students. The gallery holds over 1,500 great reproductions of icons, frescoes and miniatures from Serbian medieval monasteries and churches which together show the development of different regional icon painting schools of the period. Although this collection consists entirely of replicas, it is worth visiting because in many cases the replicas are all that are left, as the originals were damaged or totally destroyed over the centuries. The gallery often organizes exhibitions world-wide where everyone can become acquainted with the long and rich tradition of Serbia's fresco painting. The gallery is not that widely attended since it is not listed in many visitor guides. However, The Gallery of Frescoes still remains one of the most significant national and cultural treasures of Serbia.

СТУДЕНИЦА
ОСАМ ВЕКОВА СЛИКАРСТВА   EIGHT CENTURIES OF WALL PAINTING
STUDENICA

❖ *The Vuk and Dositej Museum*

This museum is located in the Dorćol district of Belgrade, in one the oldest buildings which used to be a luxurious Turkish residence. Before the museum was founded in 1949, this structure was called the Great School, and was part of the University of Belgrade, which was initially established by the great Serbian educator, Dositej Obradović. The museum is divided into two parts, each one dedicated to one of the two great Serbian scholars and educators. The first floor is dedicated to Vuk Stefanović Karadzić, one of the first students of the Great School, a prominent scholar and linguist who wrote the first Serbian dictionary, codified Serbian grammar and reformed the Serbian alphabet. The museum holds many of Vuk Karadzić's personal artifacts such as diplomas, bills, notes, attire, etc. The second floor of the building preserves the memory of Dositej Obradović, a philosopher of Enlightenment and writer who became the first Serbian Minister of Education. Unfortunately, the museum does not have an authentic and complete collection of Dositej's personal artifacts since most of his books, writings and other possessions were damaged or destroyed at the beginning of the 19th century. The museum has its own valuable library, small reading room and a collection of photographs and portraits. Thanks to the helpful staff, a visitor to the museum can get a good sense of the importance and impact that these prominent scholars had on Serbian culture.

Dositej Obradović

Vuk Karadzić

The Museum of the Serbian Orthodox Church

❖ *The Collection of the Serbian Orthodox Church*

Located in a small area in the main building of the Patriarchate in Belgrade, the museum is only a small portion of the larger collection displayed at any one time. The impressive collection of icons, manuscripts, paintings, liturgical objects, church books, original correspondence and other artifacts is quite important in cultural and historical value. Some of these items date back to the 14th century. The Serbian Orthodox Church often loans these irreplaceable objects for display to various museums and exhibitions around the world. Some of the more noteworthy items in the collection include the 14th century cape of Knez Lazar, artifacts of King Milutin, the first Serbian printed religious books, Otkoih, 15th century and Tetragospel, 16th century. Although not widely publicized, this small museum's collection is most significant culturally and historically and well worth a visit.

❖ *Vuk Karadzić's Birth Home in Tršić*

Karadzić, the great Serbian scholar and pioneer of Serbian literature, was born in Tršić, a small village in western Serbia near Loznica in the Drina River Valley. Vuk's family home in Tršić has been turned into a museum, keeping alive the memory of the eminent intellectual. The modest sized main house holds the portrait of Vuk from the 19th century, as well as a significant collection of the original household objects (dishes, pottery, furniture, gusle, etc.). After much renovation, road construction and infrastructure improvements, the village of Tršić became a "museum village" and a favorite picnic area visited by many lovers of rural tourism. Not far from Vuk's house, a popular place in the village is the Saborište (gathering place) with its amphitheater, where cultural events are held. Every year Tršić hosts a cultural festival called Vukov Sabor where visitors, enjoying a rich traditional cultural program, come to celebrate Vuk's life and work.

Aviation Museum

Arrive at the airport early for your departing flight and stop at this attractively built Aviation Museum. It houses a collection of more than 200 aircraft, 130 aircraft engines, several radar systems, missiles and aircraft equipment. The Aviation Museum, founded in 1957, is located just outside the Nikola Tesla International Airport. It has one of the world's largest collections of military aircraft, including models from both World Wars, post World War II aircraft, and more recently from NATO's attack on Serbia, (parts of F-16 and F-117 Stealth Bomber wreckage) including various downed and undetonated drone aircraft and cruise missiles. All the items are exhibited either in the museum's modern round glass building or on the adjoining grounds. As the only preserved airplane of its kind in the world, the model Fiat G-50 has a special place among the exhibited items and is considered the single most important artifact in the museum. The collection also includes helicopters, jet fighters, a passenger plane, and gliders that belonged to the Yugoslav Air Force, Yugoslav Airlines and aeronautical clubs. The museum collection also includes various radars, rockets, aeronautical equipment, over 20,000 books, documentation and more than 200,000 photographs.

1999 NATO Bombing Map

Serbia's Fight to Remain Free

Because of its geographical position, right on the border, straddling 2 worlds, Eastern and Western Christianity, along with the ever-present Muslim element, Serbia has always been under the threat of external political and religious domination. However, it should be noted that some of these threats were purely a case of geographic expansion by enemy forces such as Nazi Germany in WWII. Many years spent under occupation by different forces influenced the Serbian consciousness, instilling the idea that Serbs have to be ever vigilant and always prepared to fight for their own freedom.

The medieval Serbian state was one of the most prominent and powerful states in Europe. Under Tsar Stefan Dušan (called The Mighty), the Serbian state thrived politically and economically until the Turks invaded. In 2 crucial battles: the Battle of Marica in 1371, and the Battle of Kosovo in 1389, events initiated a steady downward spiral for Serbia and ultimately resulted in 5 centuries of Turkish Muslim occupation and enslavement. The occupying Turkish territorial administrators' ever more brutal treatment of the local civilian population caused the entire Serbian population to rise up against Ottoman rule.

Serbia's First Uprising (1804-1813) was led by Karadjordje Petrović. The Second Serbian Uprising (1815-1817) was led by Miloš Obrenović. These 2 uprisings were the initial catalyst in the formation of the modern Serbian state in the 19th century. Since then, Serbia has had to defend her freedom from Austro-Hungarian and German occupiers in the 20th century. Vastly outnumbered by the powerful Austro-Hungarian Empire, Serbia struggled to preserve her cultural life, church autonomy, and language. In WWI, Serbia as an ally of the Balkan Entente Power, contributed to the final capitulation of Austro-Hungary.

In WWII when Nazi troops occupied Serbian territory, at great cost to human life of its civilian population, Serbia managed to put up Europe's first organized resistance to Nazi Germany and eventually regained her freedom.

The reminders of foreign aggressions from every period are to be found everywhere in Serbia. Particularly moving are the Skull Tower in Niš, a monument to Serbian rebels in the First Serbian Uprising whose decapitated heads were used by the Turkish army to build the ramparts of the tower and Memorial Park in Kragujevac which witnessed the massacre, at the hands of Nazi German troops, of 7,000 Serbian citizens, many of whom were students and teachers from local schools.

More recently, in 1999, Serbia again experienced the struggle in preserving her integrity and freedom at the hands of violent foreign aggression. One of the most painful episodes was the 1999 bombing of Serbia (including downtown Belgrade) by the U.S. led NATO forces. The humanitarian pretext for this aggression has long since been discredited. Over 500 civilians perished, including 70 children. The campaign's aim, as described by NATO, was to drive the Serbian Army out of Kosovo. The bombing went on for 78 days and nights, including on Easter Sunday. The attacks were very aggressive, knocking out heating plants providing heat to high-rise apartments, hospitals and schools. The government buildings targeted had, according to locals, long since been vacated. This was a psychological terror campaign waged against the civilian population including the illegal use of cluster bombs. Many crop fields and water sources were contaminated by depleted uranium shells used against Serbia and required ecological clean up. In the end, the Serbs were told by the U.S. and its NATO allies that it was *"for their own good."* With friends like these...?

Monasteries and Churches

Serbia's Christianity and the Serbian Orthodox Church were unifying forces enabling Serbia to maintain its national identity during 5 centuries of oppressive and brutal Turkish occupation. The monasteries and churches are seemingly a part of Serbia's DNA. These magnificent creations are a textbook of sorts that chronicles Serbia's history throughout the ages. The majority of Serbian monasteries date back to the medieval times. These endowments were built on the territories that were under the rule of Serbian kings. Many of these structures and their beautiful frescoes are still preserved in their original forms while others had to be rebuilt many times due to their destruction by occupying forces. It is noteworthy that due to the prohibition of formal education by the occupying Turkish authority for almost 5 centuries, Serbian Orthodox churches were the place where books were printed and literacy among the Serbian people was maintained. Although not all Serbian people have always been there to support the Serbian Orthodox Church, she has always been there for the Serbian people. Today, many Serbian monasteries are protected by having been placed on UNESCO's list of World Heritage Sites. Unfortunately, this has not prevented some of the most significant Serbian Orthodox monasteries in Kosovo, which date back to the Middle Ages, from being under continued threat of destruction requiring an armed United Nations presence for security. Any visit to Serbia is incomplete without a visit to at least several of the more significant monasteries and churches.

St. Sava Cathedral is located next to the National Library of Serbia in a beautiful park in the Vračar area of Belgrade. It is built on the site where, it is thought, the Turkish army commander Sinan Pasha, in order to try and break the spirit of the Serbian people, burned St. Sava's mortal remains. This made the resolve of the Serbs in resisting that much stronger.

The Cathedral was originally conceived in the late 1800s but construction only began in 1923 and was interrupted several times, including World War II, the communist era, and most recently during the NATO attack on Serbia. Thankfully, construction has proceeded at a rapid pace. The exterior is mostly completed. The interior is undergoing painstaking detailed fitment of specified finishes. St. Sava Cathedral is considered the largest Orthodox Church in the world. The Cathedral is able to accommodate up to 10,000 people and, due to its height and location, has become an important landmark in Belgrade.

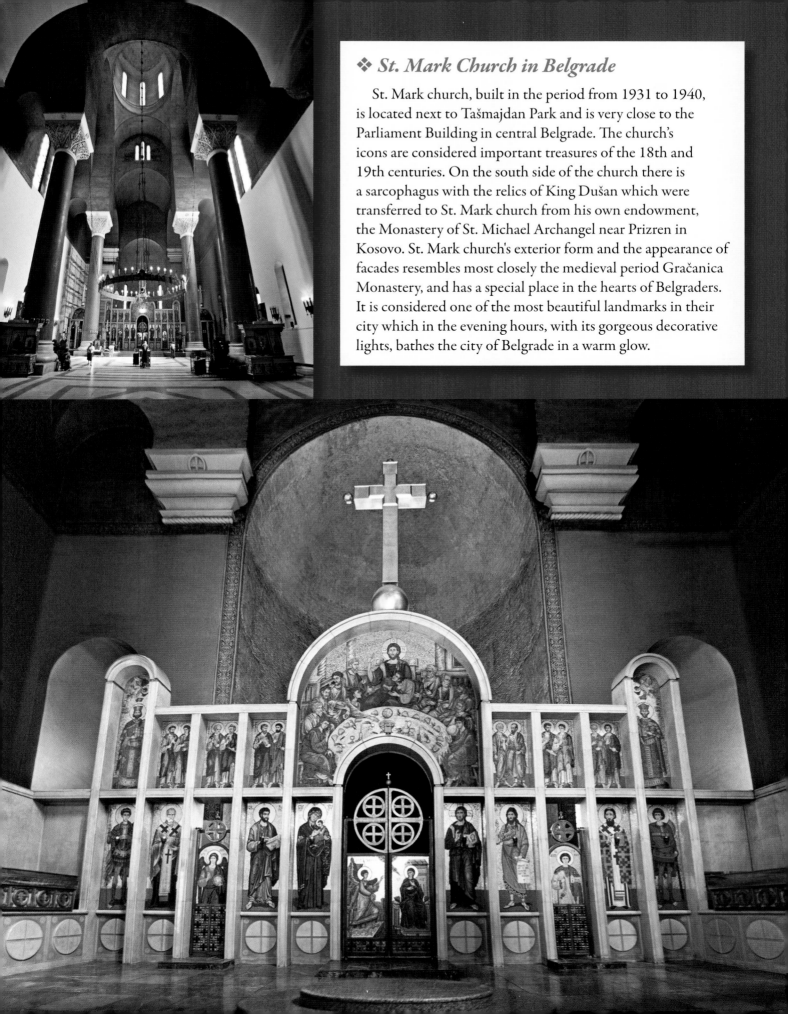

❖ *St. Mark Church in Belgrade*

St. Mark church, built in the period from 1931 to 1940, is located next to Tašmajdan Park and is very close to the Parliament Building in central Belgrade. The church's icons are considered important treasures of the 18th and 19th centuries. On the south side of the church there is a sarcophagus with the relics of King Dušan which were transferred to St. Mark church from his own endowment, the Monastery of St. Michael Archangel near Prizren in Kosovo. St. Mark church's exterior form and the appearance of facades resembles most closely the medieval period Gračanica Monastery, and has a special place in the hearts of Belgraders. It is considered one of the most beautiful landmarks in their city which in the evening hours, with its gorgeous decorative lights, bathes the city of Belgrade in a warm glow.

Mileševa Monastery

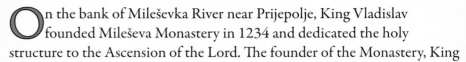

On the bank of Mileševka River near Prijepolje, King Vladislav founded Mileševa Monastery in 1234 and dedicated the holy structure to the Ascension of the Lord. The founder of the Monastery, King Vladislav, is depicted on the wall holding a model of the church in his hand. This was a typical way of portraying the rulers who endowed monasteries. It was here that the King transferred the relics of St. Sava who died on a visit to Bulgaria. Bulgarian royalty felt that Sava's earthly remains should stay in Trnovo, Bulgaria as he was related to the royal family at the time of his death. King Vladislav of Serbia negotiated for more than a year to obtain the relics of Sava which he eventually brought to Mileševa Monastery in 1236.

During this turbulent period in Serbia under Ottoman occupation, Turkish authorities moved the remains of St. Sava and had them burned on Vračar Hill in Belgrade believing that they could destroy the spirit of the Serbian people. Today St. Sava remains the most important figure of the Serbian Orthodox Church. King Vladislav himself was also laid to rest at Mileševa.

Mileševa is also an important monastery as it is where some of the most important fresco paintings of the 13th century are located. On the northern wall is a fresco of King Vladislav and on the northeastern wall of the old narthex are images of St. Simeon, St. Sava as well as Kings Stefan the First Crowned, Radoslav and Vladislav. It is important to note that the frescoes of King Vladislav and St. Sava were painted during their lifetime providing history with realistic portraits that rank among the best of the 13th century.

The monastery is equally recognized as an important printing center at the time of the Turkish occupation. Monks brought printing equipment from Venice, Italy and in 1544 printed a Psalter and a prayer book in 1545. The museum on the grounds of the monastery houses many important collections: icons, chalices, textiles, jewelry, paintings and artifacts of the early church.

In addition to the significance of its being the original resting place of St. Sava, the monastery has a number of other important frescoes as well including the well known White Angel (a detail from the composition of the myrrh-bearing women), Judas' Betrayal in the old narthex and The Taking Down from the Cross, a detail in the nave.

The fresco below of St. Sava is believed to be the last image painted of him just prior to his death. At right is the tomb of St. Sava and the relics of his hand.

❖ *Ravanica Monastery*

The Monastery of Ravanica and its church of the Ascension of the Lord holds an important place in Serbia's medieval history. The monastery not only played a historic role in the religious history of Serbia but was instrumental in the development of Serbian architecture and represents the beginning of the "Moravian School" of architecture in Serbia. Important ornamental sculpture and painting at this site are considered cultural treasures of the Serbian people. Ravanica was built in 1375 by Prince Lazar near the town of Ćuprija in central Serbia. He was killed in the Battle of Kosovo in 1389 and was canonized by the Serbian Orthodox Church in 1390. His body was carried from Kosovo to Ravanica where his earthly remains are located inside this beautiful and impressive structure. For those who consider Knez Lazar the symbol of the struggle of the Serbian Orthodox faith, tradition and history, Ravanica Monastery has become a pilgrimage landmark and the focal point around which developed the cult of the martyr Prince and the heroes of Kosovo who had fought with him.

❖ *Studenica Monastery*

Stefan Nemanja, the unifier of the Serbian states, established Studenica Monastery in the late 12th century. Stefan Nemanja relinquished his crown for the monastic life and took the name Simeon. Studenica, located south of Kraljevo on a beautiful wooded hillside near the Ušće-Ibar valley is one of Serbia's most important monasteries. The mortal relics of St. Simeon were transferred from Hilandar Monastery on Mt. Athos in modern day Greece by his son, St. Sava, and laid to rest in Studenica Monastery. Upon Sava's return from Hilandar at the beginning of the13th century, this monastery was frescoed on his initiative. Studenica's frescoes at that time represented a novelty never before seen in Serbia. As far as sculptural decoration is concerned, for a long time Studenica served as an accepted building model for churches in Medieval Serbia. Under St. Sava's guardianship Studenica became the political, spiritual and cultural center of Serbia. The complex of Studenica Monastery includes the Church of the Holy Virgin, the Church of St. Nicholas, and the King's Church. Beside these churches there is one small museum, and a monastic residence dating back to the 18th century, where many precious artifacts of Studenica's treasure are kept.

❖ Visoki Dečani Monastery

Dečani Monastery is located in Metohija, under the Prokletije Mountains, south of Peć, in the Bistrica River valley. The building of the church, dedicated to Christ Pantocrator, commenced in 1327, during the reign of King Stefan Dečanski, and was completed in 1335 by his son Emperor Dušan Silni. Visoki Dečani is the largest and tallest of the church endowments of Medieval Serbia. With its outstanding frescoes and exceptionally detailed design elements and a part of the Raška style group of monuments, Visoki Dečani represents the peak of Serbian iconography. Although the monastery has suffered damage and has been rebuilt a number of times during its existence, the beautiful 14th century frescoes have been completely preserved. On its walls is depicted the Nemanjić genealogical tree. Stefan Dečanski, who was buried next to the iconostasis, is portrayed holding the church model in his hands, which was the traditional way of presenting the patrons of the church. Visoki Dečani was and still is a very important spiritual and cultural center for the Serbian people. In 2004 Visoki Dečani Monastery was placed on UNESCO's World Heritage List. Today 30 young, gifted monks live in the monastery meticulously engaged in various artistic activities such as wood carving, icon painting and book publishing.

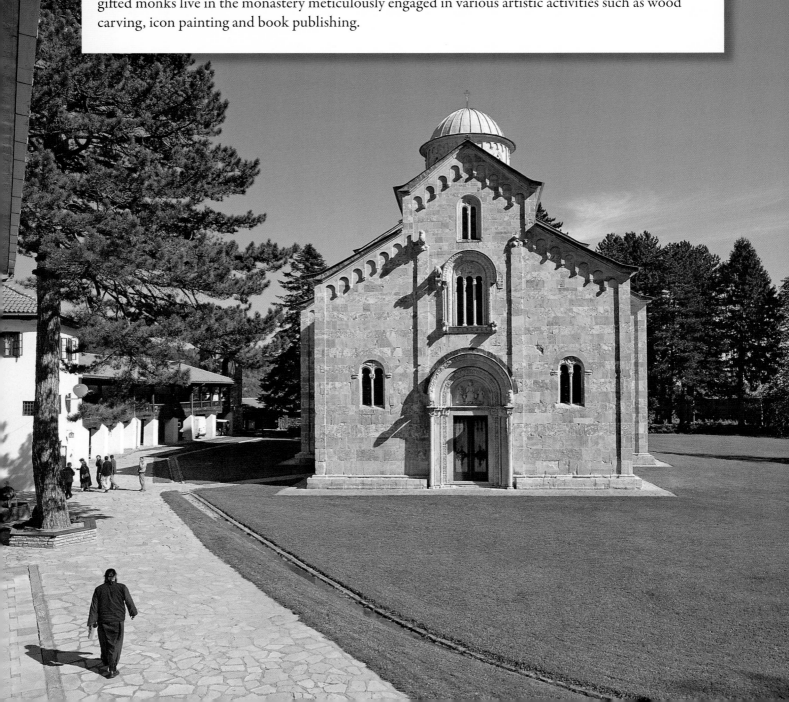

The Church of St. Apostles Peter and Paul, located near Novi Pazar, dates to the 8th century and was built on the foundation of a church originally built in the 4th century, it is the oldest Orthodox Christian church in Serbia.

Multi-Religious Tolerance in Serbia

As one walks around Belgrade, you are struck by the variety of the different houses of worship. In addition to the images shown here of a Roman Catholic church, a synagogue and a mosque, there are several other Roman Catholic churches in Belgrade as well as a Russian Orthodox, a Protestant, a Baptist and an Adventist church.

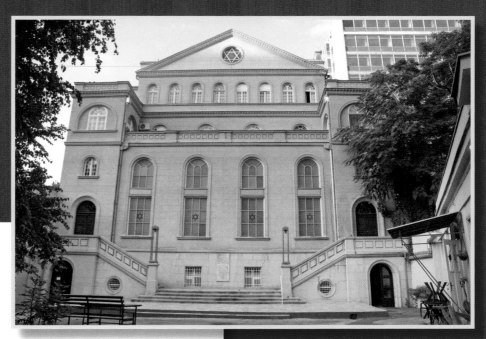

Kragujevac

City of History, Industry and Sorrow

Located less than 100 miles south of Belgrade in the heart of the Šumadija region, is a city of industry with about 200,000 inhabitants. Well known as the focal point of Serbia's automobile industry (Zastava), Kragujevac is also an educational and cultural center of central Serbia. For a brief period in the early 1800s, Kragujevac was the capital city of Serbia under Knez Miloš Obrenović. This city, through which the Lepenica River flows, is the home of Serbia's many firsts such as: the first capital city of the modern Serbian state, the first Serbian city with an electricity generating plant, the first court, the first modern high school and the first theatre.

More recently, in the Second World War, Kragujevac was the location of an extremely brutal campaign by Nazi Germany against the civilian population; many of its citizens were executed including children, students and teachers. Two of Kragujevac's best known landmarks are connected to this brutal episode; the Memorial Park and the Museum 21st October.

Currently, Kragujevac is experiencing a renaissance of its traditional role as Serbia's industrial center. Most noteworthy is the arrival of FIAT, solidifying a growing auto industry and including all the related component manufacturing and supply networks.

Top: The main Serbian Orthodox church in Kragujevac is located near the city center. Bishop Jovan who heads this Serbia Diocese served as the Bishop of the American Western Diocese in Los Angeles for several years before returning to Serbia. *Bottom:* A church under construction in Male Pčelice, on the outskirts of Kragujevac is representative of many church construction projects currently underway throughout Serbia.

The statue of Vuk Karadzić sits in front of the first gymnasium (high school) built in Kragujevac after nearly 5 centuries of Turkish occupation during which time Serbians were denied the right to an education.

Ratomir

Draga

Ratomir, from Gornja Šatornja near Rudnik, still has very vivid memories from his youth as a soldier during WWII when he was defending his homeland. Listening to the vivid details of battles at specific locations, one has the impression that the experiences he is sharing occurred only a few days prior rather than having taken place more than sixty years ago. These days he operates his small farm with the help of his family and is particularly proud of his homemade plum and apricot brandy (rakija). The thing he looks forward to most these days are summers, because that's when his son and granddaughters visit him from the United States.

Draga, the middle child of three born to Marina and Božidar, was born in Male Pčelice, near Kragujevac, in the early 1930s. She and her husband Pavle and two children emigrated to the United States in the late 1960s. After retirement, Draga and Pavle built a new house in Male Pčelice on the same spot where their old house was located. They spend summers in Male Pčelice at their new house, where their four grandchildren come to visit them, and then they return to the United States each fall to be with their children and grandchildren for Slava, Christmas, New Year and Easter.

Kragujevac Memorial Park

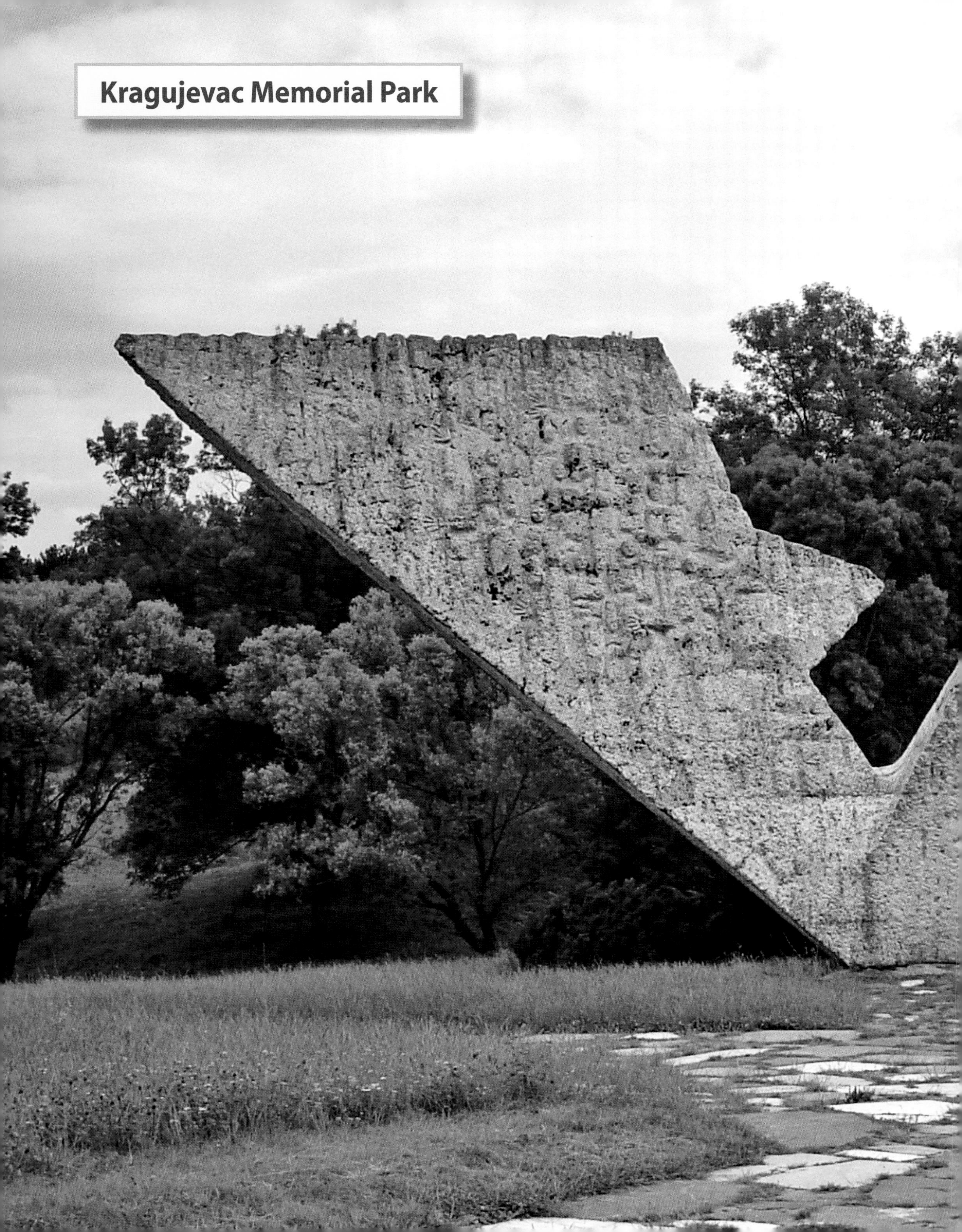

❖ *Memorial Park – Spomen Park*

In October of 1941 Kragujevac experienced a tragedy of epic proportions when approximately 7,000 of its citizens were brutally executed by the occupying German Nazis. Many of the victims were children, students and their teachers. The park encompasses the area which includes 30 mass grave sites. The two most recognizable monuments are the monument dedicated to the executed students and teachers which is in the shape of a giant letter "V" and the monument dedicated to "Pain and Defiance" which is a chiseled image of two individuals falling down after being shot. The Memorial Park and the adjoining Museum 21st October are very moving reminders of a distressing recent past.

"If my life is in your hands then I don't need it"

—Fr. Andreja Božić

On October 21st, 1941, the first group of prisoners were held by occupying Nazi forces in the King Petar School and subsequently executed at this location—among them was Fr. Andreja.

Museum 21st October

Located at the entrance to the Memorial Park is the Museum 21st October. The museum, including its architectural design, is dedicated to the approximate 7,000 unarmed civilian victims who were executed during October, 1941, by the occupying German Nazi troops. The building's appearance itself tells a tragic story in symbols. From the outside the building appears to look like 30 silos placed one next to another with no windows. The lack of windows symbolizes the inability of unarmed individuals to escape the machine gun barrels. The 30 silos, like peaks, are a reminder of the 30 mass graves where the executed were shot and buried. The tops of the silos are clear windows which represent the victims' last look at the sky as they fell to the ground. The museum is movingly presented and evokes great emotion.

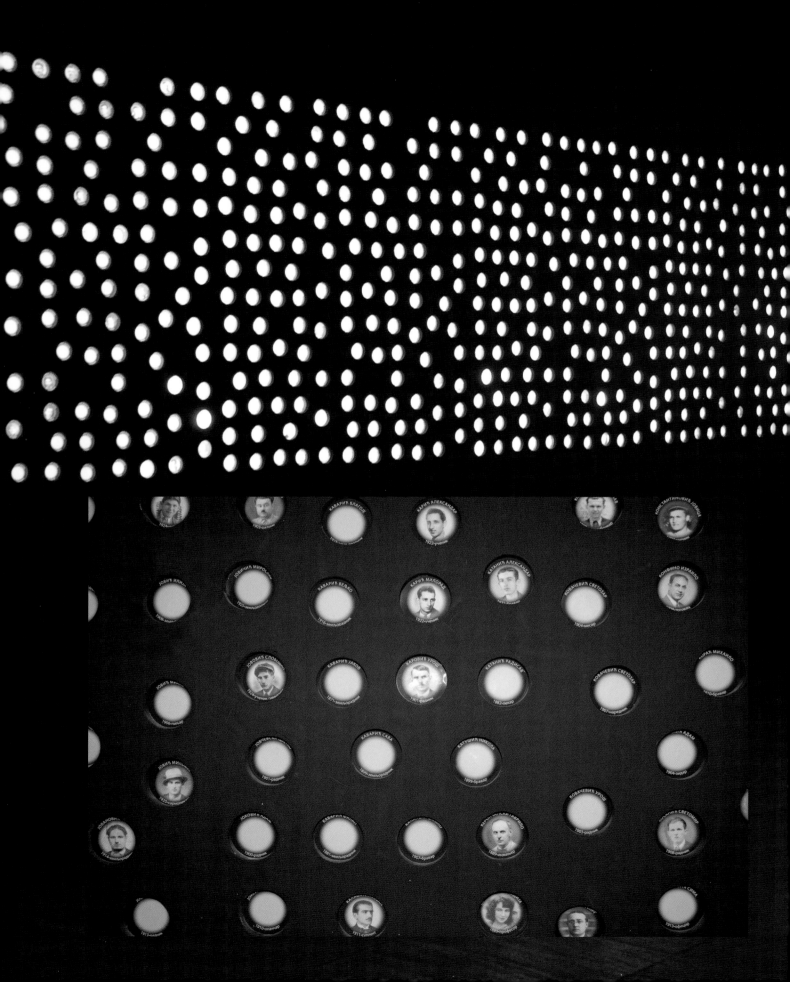

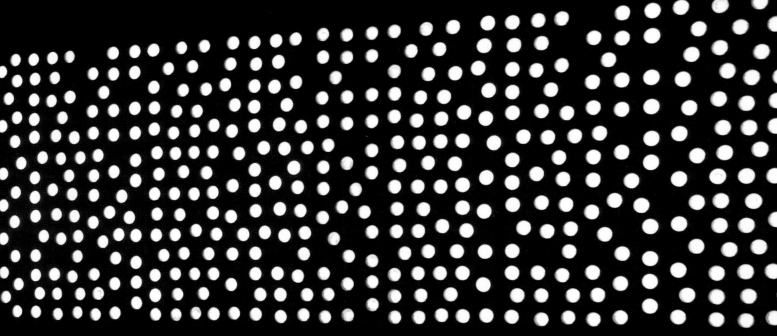

ЈОВАНОВИЋ МИЛОРАД
1895•професор

The Victims in Kragujevac

In the central hall on the ground floor of the museum you approach what looks as though its walls are decorated with illuminated circular objects. The illuminated elements are evenly spaced covering 2 entire walls, nearly floor to ceiling.

It is only once one has walked up close to the walls that it becomes apparent what the lights actually are. Each backlit opening identifies an executed victim—with their image, name, year of birth and profession. For the several thousand victims whose remains were never identified, the backlit opening has been left blank. The room is one of the most moving and somber places in the museum.

As Serbia's third largest city Niš has, a population in excess of 250,000 inhabitants. The city is an important industrial center and the location of a major university with a student body exceeding 25,000.

Although there is archeological evidence that settlements in and around the areas occupied by current day Niš were present as far back as perhaps 5,000 BC, it was during the time of the Roman Empire that Niš, or Nassius as the Romans called it, became a prominent and important city. Niš was one of the key cities connected by Rome's first century Via Militaris road network where 5 roads converged.

In addition to being the birthplace of the first Christian Roman Emperor, Constantine the Great for whom its international airport is named, Niš is also the birthplace of Roman emperors Constantius III and Justin I.

The city, which prospered under the Romans, was conquered and its inhabitants massacred by Attila the Hun in the year 443. The Romans re-conquered Niš, but the city never quite achieved its old prominence or prosperity. Starting in the latter half of the 6th century, it took the Slavic tribes 8 attempts to conquer Niš during which time most of the Roman population evacuated the area. From the 7th century on, Niš has been controlled by many occupying forces such as the Bulgarians, Hungarians and the Byzantine Empire, with the Serbians finally incorporating Niš into their state in the 12th century. From 1375 until its liberation in the 19th century Niš was captured by Ottoman Turks and liberated by the Serbians and Austrians several times. The brutality of Turkish rule can be illustrated by Niš' unique Skull Tower (Ćele Kula) monument constructed from the skulls of

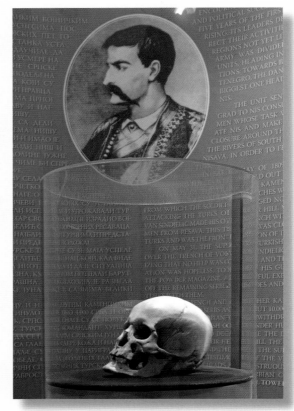

decapitated freedom-fighters who rose up in opposition. In the central part of Niš one can still see the original Turkish fort built in the 1700s.

In the 20th century Niš was occupied in WWI and WWII by Austria, Bulgaria and Germany. More recently in 1999, Niš was the location of NATO cluster bombings which resulted in many civilian casualties but no military losses.

In recognition of the significance to Christianity due to the birth of Constantine the Great, in 2013 Niš will host the Ecumenical Assembly of Christian Churches in honor of 1700 years since Constantine's Edict of Milan.

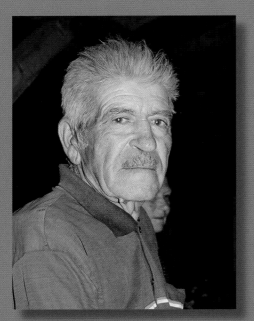

Sveto

Sveto lives in Grajevci, a small village near Leskovac. He was a bricklayer before retiring. Now, as well as prior to retirement, Sveto runs a small family farm. He and his wife have a son and a daughter. His daughter and her family live in Australia. His son, a civil engineer, and his family live nearby.

Željko

Željko lives in Niš, where he is a police officer, but was assigned to work for one month in Belgrade as part of the security detail during the 2009 university games (Univerzijada) for events such as the marathon race. As nice as the experience in Belgrade has been for Željko, he could not wait to go back home to see his two young sons.

Mara

Mara lived in Leskovac. She recently passed away. Everybody remembers her as a lady who always was in a good mood and displayed a good sense of humor. A lasting image of Mara is that of her going to the market or running other errands on her bicycle.

Ratka

Ratka was a very proud lady who lived in Vlasotince near her son, grandson and great grandchildren until her recent passing. Although she was happy to be around her family, she missed her sister and friends who had passed away. She rarely had an opportunity to see her sister who lives in Belgrade or another sister and brother who live in the U.S. Sadly, to her, they all seemed equally far away.

Novi Sad

As Serbia's second largest city, Novi Sad has a population near 300,000 and a metropolitan area approaching 400,000. The city is on the southern Pannonian Plain in close proximity to the Fruška Gora Mountains and on the banks of the Danube River. It is the administrative center of the Vojvodina province. The city was originally settled on the right bank of the Danube where today sits its most recognized structure, the impressive Petrovaradin Fortress. Petrovaradin, which sits high on the banks of the Danube, is a real engineering marvel and an important historical structure. The majority of inhabitants, however, live and work across the river where the current day residential and commercial hub of Novi Sad is located.

As with most of the Balkans, this area was subject to being overrun by invading armies and over its history has been ruled by the Celts, Romans, Huns, Goths, Avars, Franks, Bulgarians, Byzantines, Hungarians, Ottoman Turks, Germans, and of course currently is part of Serbia. Although there is evidence of early settlements in the area as far back as 4,500 BC and the Slavs have been in the area since the 6th century, the city was officially founded by Serbians in 1694. The ethnic Hungarians mostly abandoned the area in and around Novi Sad during the rule of the Ottoman Turks, leaving it predominantly Serbian. The 18th and 19th centuries saw the city become the largest city in the world inhabited by Serbs and an important commercial center which was almost completely destroyed in the Revolution in 1848. The city was slowly restored, becoming an important cultural hub earning its informal name as the Serbian Athens. It should be noted that during this period virtually every Serbian writer and poet lived in Novi Sad for some period of time and that it was this period when Matica Srpska, Serbia's oldest cultural and scientific institution was moved to Novi Sad from Budapest. Its library today contains almost a million books.

During this period, Novi Sad was located in the Hungarian part of the Austro-Hungarian Empire, and was subject to the Hungarians Magyarization policy which dramatically changed the demographics of Novi Sad resulting in the Serbs being the majority, but with a substantial

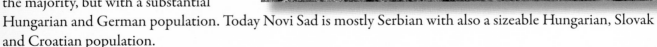

Hungarian and German population. Today Novi Sad is mostly Serbian with also a sizeable Hungarian, Slovak and Croatian population.

In 1918, after WWI, the Assembly of Vojvodina proclaimed a union with the Kingdom of Serbia. In WWII, Novi Sad saw a period of brutal occupation by the Nazis where many thousands were killed.

After the war, rapid industrialization and population growth saw Novi Sad prosper until the 1990s sanctions and the 1999 NATO bombing which destroyed Novi Sad's bridges and infrastructure, causing great economic and ecological damage.

The city has recovered and has become an important financial, commercial and educational center with numerous banks, large companies and 2 major universities. Since 2001, one of Europe's most popular music festivals called *EXIT*, is held by the Petrovaradin Fortress.

JANIKA BALAŽ
1925 - 1988

JOBAH
JOBAHOBИЋ
ЗМАЈ

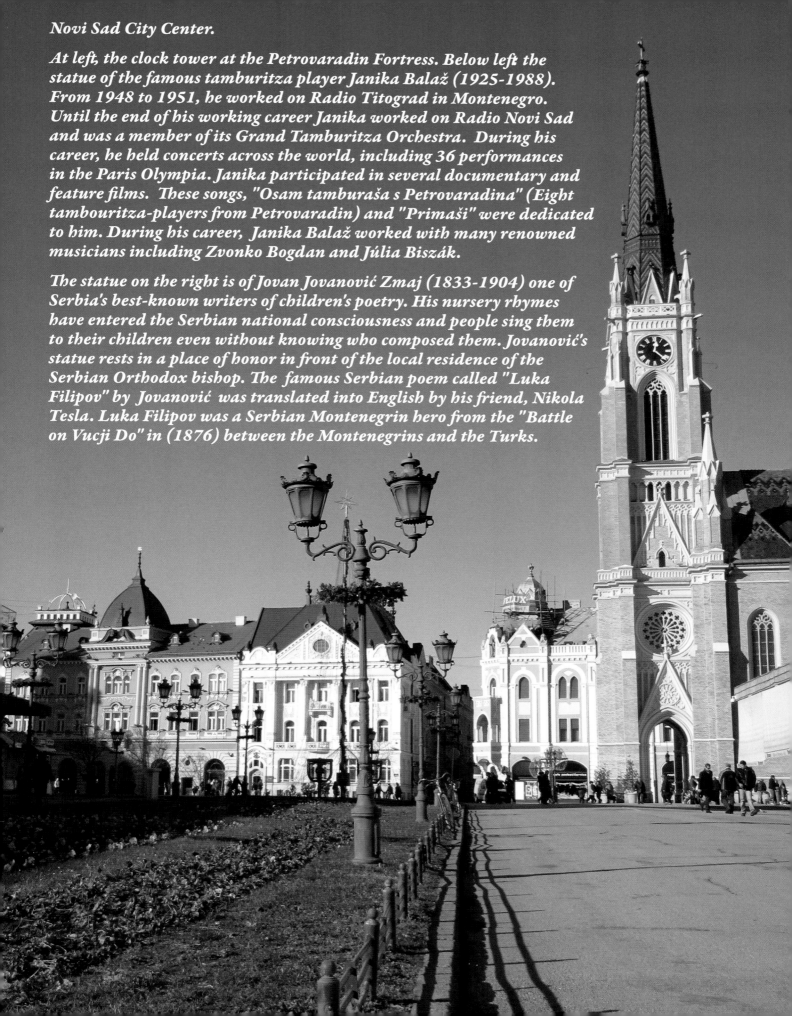

Novi Sad City Center.

At left, the clock tower at the Petrovaradin Fortress. Below left the statue of the famous tamburitza player Janika Balaž (1925-1988). From 1948 to 1951, he worked on Radio Titograd in Montenegro. Until the end of his working career Janika worked on Radio Novi Sad and was a member of its Grand Tamburitza Orchestra. During his career, he held concerts across the world, including 36 performances in the Paris Olympia. Janika participated in several documentary and feature films. These songs, "Osam tamburaša s Petrovaradina" (Eight tambouritza-players from Petrovaradin) and "Primaši" were dedicated to him. During his career, Janika Balaž worked with many renowned musicians including Zvonko Bogdan and Júlia Biszák.

The statue on the right is of Jovan Jovanović Zmaj (1833-1904) one of Serbia's best-known writers of children's poetry. His nursery rhymes have entered the Serbian national consciousness and people sing them to their children even without knowing who composed them. Jovanović's statue rests in a place of honor in front of the local residence of the Serbian Orthodox bishop. The famous Serbian poem called "Luka Filipov" by Jovanović was translated into English by his friend, Nikola Tesla. Luka Filipov was a Serbian Montenegrin hero from the "Battle on Vucji Do" in (1876) between the Montenegrins and the Turks.

Subotica

Situated on Serbia's northern border, Subotica is Serbia's fifth largest city with a population of approximately 150,000 inhabitants. It is Serbia's most ethnically and religiously diverse city.

The earliest recorded reference to the city dates back to the late 1300s. Because of its location, Subotica has seen many different peoples come through over the years and it is said to be the reason it is believed that there are perhaps as many as 200 different names for Subotica through the ages. The first settlements most likely took place in the mid 1200s as a result of people pouring in whose nearby villages were destroyed during the Tatar invasions.

Subotica gradually became a frontier town of the Ottoman Empire in the 1500s. By this time, the majority of the town's Hungarian population had fled north toward Hungary. The Ottoman Turks ruled the town from the mid 1500s until the late 1600s. During this period the Turks encouraged new settlers to come to the area. As it happened, most of the new settlers were Orthodox Serbs. In 1697, Subotica became part of the Hapsburg Monarchy after the defeat of the Turks. As a result of the service to the Hapsburg Monarchy in expelling the Turks, Serb military families were given certain privileges.

With the establishment of the dual monarchy in the mid 1800s, Subotica had built its landmark theatre, opened many schools and was connected to a main rail line. In the late 1800s an electric power plant was built as well. Subotica remained a part of the Austro-Hungarian Empire until the end of WWI in 1918, when it became a part of *The Kingdom of Serbs, Croats and Slovenes* at which time it was the third largest city in the country.

Evidence of Subotica's diversity can be seen in the different houses of worship—including a synagogue. Of the churches, there are two Orthodox, two Protestant, a Lutheran and a Calvinist.

In close geographic proximity to Subotica is the well known resort area of Palić and its lake. Palić hosts many festivals, fairs and exhibits. It is a high quality recreational area with hotels and restaurants.

Serbia is Big on Small Business

Serbians Love to Party

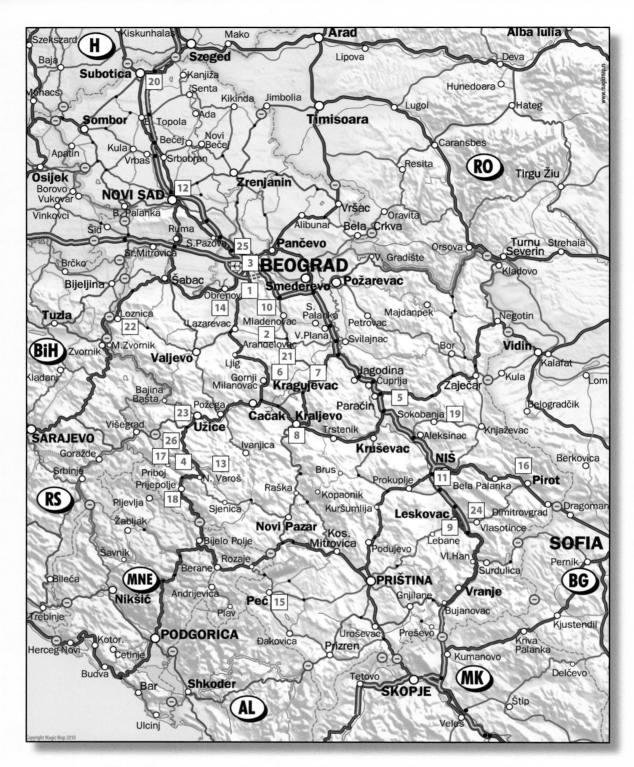

The places mentioned in this book represent a diverse geographic
and socioeconomic sampling of Serbia.

1 Avala	**8** Kraljevo	**15** Peć	**22** Tršić
2 Arandjelovac	**9** Leskovac	**16** Pirot	**23** Užice
3 Belgrade	**10** Mladenovac	**17** Priboj	**24** Vlasotince
4 Bistrica	**11** Niš	**18** Prijepolje	**25** Zemun
5 Ćuprija/Jagodina	**12** Novi Sad	**19** Sokobanja	**26** Zlatibor
6 Gornja Šatornja	**13** Nova Varoš	**20** Subotica	
7 Kragujevac	**14** Obrenovac	**21** Topola	

Profile of Serbia

The following basic profile, including the statistical information, whose source is the official web site of the Republic of Serbia, can be found at www.srbija.gov.rs and www.serbiaembusa.org.

The Republic of Serbia is a democratic state for all of its citizens. Its history and achievements make it an integral part of modern civilization.

Apart from Serbia Proper, the Republic of Serbia contains two autonomous provinces: Vojvodina and Kosovo-Metohija. Belgrade is the capital of Serbia. With a population of almost two million, it is the country's administrative, economic and cultural centre.

Population, Language and Religion

The ethnic composition of the population of the Republic of Serbia is very diverse, which is a result of the country's turbulent past. The majority of the population of Serbia are Serbs, but another 37 ethnicities also live on its territory. All citizens have equal rights and responsibilities and enjoy full ethnic equality.

The Constitution of the Republic of Serbia guarantees rights to minorities, in accordance with the highest international standards. The latest 2002 census puts the population of Serbia (excluding Kosovo-Metohija) at 7,498,001, which makes up 92.3% of the population of the former State Union of Serbia-Montenegro. Serbs make up 82.86% of the population, Hungarians 3.91%, Bosniaks 1.81%, Roma 1.44%, Yugoslavs 1.08%, Croats 0.94%, Montenegrins 0.92%, Albanians 0.82%, Slovaks 0.79%, Vlachs 0.53%, Romanians 0.46%, Macedonians 0.34%, Bulgarians and Vojvodina Croats 0.27% each, Muslims 0.26%, Ruthenians 0.21%, Slovaks and Ukrainians .07% each, Gorani 0.06%, Germans 0.05%, and Russians and Czechs 0.03% each.

The official language in Serbia is Serbian and the script in official use is Cyrillic, while Latin script is also used. In the areas inhabited by ethnic minorities, the languages and scripts of the minorities are in official use, as provided by law.

The main religion of Serbia is Orthodox Christian, the faith of the Serbian people. The Serbian Orthodox Church, which has been autonomous since 1219, has played an important role in the development and preservation of the Serbian national identity. As well as the Christian Orthodox population, there are also other religious communities in Serbia: Islamic, Roman Catholic, Protestant, Jewish and others.

Position, Territory and Climate

Serbia is located in the central part of the Balkan Peninsula, on the most important route linking Europe and Asia, occupying an area of 88, 361 sq. km. Serbia is in the West European time zone (one hour ahead of Greenwich Time). Its climate is temperate continental, with a gradual transition between the four seasons of the year.

Serbia is referred to as the crossroads of Europe. The international roads and railways passing down its river valleys make up the shortest link between Western and Central Europe, on the one side, and the Middle East, Asia and Africa, on the other. Hence, there is great geopolitical importance to its territory. These roads follow the course of the valley of the river Morava, splitting in two near the city of Niš. One track follows the valleys of the rivers Southern Morava and Vardar to Thessaloniki; the other, the river Nišava to Sofia and Istanbul.

Serbian rivers belong to the basins of the Black, Adriatic and Aegean Seas. Three of them, the Danube, Sava and Tisa, are navigable. The longest river is the Danube, which flows for 588 of its 2,857 kilometer course through Serbia. The Danube basin has always been important for Serbia. With the commissioning of the Rhine-Main-Danube Canal in September 1992, the Black Sea and the near and Far Eastern ports have come much nearer to Europe. Serbia is linked to the Adriatic Sea and Montenegro via Belgrade-Bar railway.

Northern Serbia is mainly flat, while its central and southern areas consist of highlands and mountains. The flatlands are mainly in Vojvodina (the Pannonian Plain and its rim: Mačva, the Sava Valley, the Morava Valley, Stig and the Negotin Marshes in Eastern Serbia). 55 percent of Serbia is arable land, and 27 percent is forested. Of its mountains 15 reach heights of over 2,000 meters, the highest being Djeravica in the Prokletija range (2,656 m).

The length of Serbia's border is 2,114.2 km. To the east Serbia borders with Bulgaria, to the northeast with Romania, to the north with Hungary, to the west with Croatia and Bosnia and Herzegovina, to the southwest with Montenegro and to the south with Albania and Macedonia.

Statistics

Basic statistical data on Serbia (according to the census from 2002)
Territory: 88,361 km$_2$
Location: Between 41°52' and 46°11' of North latitude and 18°06' and 23°01'
          of East longitude
Population (excluding Kosovo): 7,498,001

Largest Cities (over 100,000 inhabitants)

CITY	NUMBER OF CITIZENS
Belgrade	1.576.124
Novi Sad	299.294
Niš	250.518
Kragujevac	175.802

Longest Rivers

RIVER	LENGTH
Danube	588 km (total 2783 km)
Zapadna Morava	308 km (308 km)
Južna Morava	295 km (295 km)
Ibar	272 km (272 km)
Drina	220 km (346 km)
Sava	206 km (945 km)
Timok	202 km (202 km)
Velika Morava	185 km (185 km)
Tisa	168 km (966 km)
Nišava	151 km (218 km)
Tamiš	118 km (359 km)
Begej	75 km (244 km)

Highest Mountain Peaks

PEAK	HEIGHT
Deravica	2,656 m (on mountain Prokletije)
Crni Vrh	2,585 m (Šar-mountain)
Gušam	2,539 m (Prokletije)
Bogdaš	2,533 m (Prokletije)
Žuti Kamen	2,522 m (Prokletije)
Ljuboten	2,498 m (Šar-mountain)
Veternik	2,461 m (Koprivnik)
Crni Krš	2,426 m (Prokletije)
Hajla	2,403 m (Hajla)

Total length of railway network
3,619 km
Total length of roads
42,692 km (asphalt) and 24,860 km (concrete)
Agricultural land
5,718,599 ha out of which:
· 4,674,622 ha arable land,
· 1,006,473 ha pastures,
· 37,504 ha fish-ponds.

Sown with:
· 2,453,374 ha Cereals
· 494,598 ha Reed-marshes and ponds forage
· 348,641 ha Industrial herbs
· 300,484 ha Vegetables
· 256,887 ha Orchards
· 85,763 ha Vineyards
· 2,164 ha Nursery-gardens
· 64,722 ha Not cultivated
· 666,702 ha Meadows
· 86,866 ha Forests

Photo Credits

Cover: Katarina Stafanović

Insets: Branislav Strugar

5	Branislav Strugar
6-7	Branislav Strugar
8	Branislav Strugar
10-11	Katarina Stafanović
12	Katarina Stafanović
14	*Girl with cup,* Russell Gordon
	Bill Dorich
15	Katarina Stafanović
16	Bill Dorich
18-19	Val Rajić, Bill Dorich
	Dragana Seizović, Ivana Rajić
	Boy with Squash, Russell Gordon
20-21	Val Rajić, Bill Dorich,
	Dragana Seizović
22	Val Rajić,
	Families with eggs, Russell Gordon
23	Katarina Stafanović
24-25	Val Rajić
26	Russell Gordon,
	Child, Dragana Seizović
27	Val Rajić, Background
	Insets, Russell Gordon
28	Branislav Strugar
29	Katarina Stafanović
30	Branislav Strugar
31	Val Rajić, Bill Dorich,
	Dragana Seizović
32-33	Bill Dorich
34	Val Rajić
35	Katarina Stafanović
36-37	Val Rajić
38	Katarina Stafanović
39	Val Rajić
40-41	Val Rajić
42-43	Bill Dorich
44	Val Rajić
45	Bill Dorich,
	lake view, Branislav Strugar
46-47	Bill Dorich
48-49	Val Rajić, Dragana Seizović
50-51	Bill Dorich
52-53	Bill Dorich
54-55	Russell Gordon
56	Russell Gordon
57	Branislav Strugar
58	*Top Right,* Branislav Strugar
	Bill Dorich
59	Katarina Stafanović
60-61	Branislav Strugar
62	*Top,* Branislav Strugar
	Bottom, Val Rajić
63	Katarina Stefanović
64	Val Rajić,
65	Bill Dorich
66	Katarina Stefanović
67	Branislav Strugar
68-69	Russell Gordon
70-71	Bill Dorich
72	Furnished by subject
73	Courtesy of the (NBA)
	National Basketball Assoc.
74	*Top,* Furnished by subject
	Bottom, Bill Dorich
75	*Left,* Val Rajić
	Right, Furnished by artist
76-77	Bill Dorich
78-79	Bill Dorich
80	*Left,* Furnished by subjects
	Right Bill Dorich
80	*Right,* Bill Dorich
81	Bill Dorich, Val Rajić
82-83	Bill Dorich
84	Val Rajić
85	Val Rajić
	Musician top right, Russell Gordan
86-87	Bill Dorich
	Insets, Vlada Marinković
88	*Left,* Bill Dorich
	Right, RTS - Radio Television Serbia
89	*Left,* Bill Dorich
	Right, Val Rajić
90-91	Val Rajić
92	Val Rajić
93	Vlada Marinković
94-95	Val Rajić
96	Igor Jeremić
97	Katarina Stafanović
98	Val Rajić

Photo Credits

About the Authors

Vladeta (Val) Rajić was born in Serbia. He started his elementary school education in Serbia but soon thereafter his family immigrated to the United States, settling in Chicago, Illinois. He completed his university undergraduate studies at the University of Illinois, earning a Bachelors of Science degree in Accounting. Mr. Rajić also holds a Masters of Business Administration degree in Corporate Finance from the University of Dallas and is a Certified Public Accountant. He has spent virtually his entire career in the financial services industry with leading firms in the insurance and banking sectors. Mr. Rajić has traveled extensively through Europe, including many visits to his native Serbia. These visits were for him, and continue to be, an opportunity to be a student of his native culture and its people rather than as mere tourist.

Bill Dorich is a first generation American, his father was born in the Krajina. Bill was a correspondent for *The American Srbobran* for over a decade. As the founder of GM Books in 1984, he was considered a pioneer in self-publishing and has produced and published over 175 titles including *Witness to War: Images of the Persian Gulf War* for the Los Angeles Times which won a Pulitzer Prize. Mr. Dorich is author of 5 books on Balkan history including his 1992 book *Kovovo* which raised over $200,000 to aid Serbian orphans in the recent Civil Wars in former Yugoslavia. A recipient of *The Order of St. Sava* bestowed on him by the Holy Synod of Serbian Orthodox bishops and an *Award of Merit* from the Serbian Bar Association of America. He has authored three new books, *Defeat Foreclosure, The Nursing Home Crisis and Sleep Seekers* in addition to his work on *Serbia: Faces & Places*.